THE VEGAN
GOURMET

FULL FLAVOR &
VARIETY WITH
OVER 120
DELICIOUS
RECIPES

Expanded 2nd Edition

Susann Geiskopf-Hadler
Mindy Toomay

PRIMA PUBLISHING

We dedicate this book to everyone who understands that healthy
eating and fine dining can be one and the same thing.

PRIMA PUBLISHING and its colophon are trademarks of Prima Communications, Inc.

Cover photograph © 1994, Kent Lacin Media Services

Nutritional Analyses:
A per serving nutritional breakdown is provided for each recipe. If a range is given for an ingredient amount, the breakdown is based on the smaller number. If a range is given for servings, the breakdown is based on the larger number. If a choice of ingredients is given in an ingredient listing, the breakdown is calculated using the first choice. Nutritional content may vary depending on the specific brands or types of ingredients used. "Optional" ingredients or those for which no specific amount is stated are not included in the breakdown. Nutritional figures are rounded to the nearest whole number.

Geiskopf-Hadler, Susann
    The vegan gourmet, expanded 2nd edition : full flavor & variety with over 120 delicious recipes / Susann Geiskopf-Hadler, Mindy Toomay.
    p. cm.
    Includes bibliographical references and index.
    ISBN 0-7615-1626-3
    1. Vegan cookery. I. Toomay, Mindy. II. Title.
TX837.G383   1995
641.5′636—dc21   98-39841
                                          CIP

99 00 01 02 03 AA 10 9 8 7 6 5 4 3 2
Printed in the United States of America

How to Order
Single copies may be ordered from Prima Publishing, P.O. Box 1260BK, Rocklin, CA 95677; telephone (916) 632-4400. Quantity discounts are also available. On your letterhead, include information concerning the intended use of the books and the number of books you wish to purchase.

Visit us online at www.primalife.com

CONTENTS

ACKNOWLEDGMENTS

Every book is a team effort. Thank you all: Jennifer Basye Sander, who nurtured the idea along; Andi Reese Brady, who calmly and capably guided the project, really heard our ideas, and brought them to life in the finished book; Jane Gilligan, who shed light on some important issues; Laurie Anderson, who came up with lively illustrations and a lovely page design; Janet Hansen, who lays out our books with such care; and Lindy Dunlavey and associates at The Dunlavey Studio, who created a cover that portrays the beauty and sophistication of vegetables.

INTRODUCTION

* * * * * * * * *

FOR A VARIETY OF REASONS, MORE and more people are choosing to minimize or even eliminate meat, fish, dairy products, and eggs from their daily diets. But, some readers may ask, what else will really taste good and satisfy my hunger? We have attempted with this book to put such questions to rest by providing tantalizing, healthful, and hearty recipes for every meal of the day.

Nature's abundance of vegetables and fruits, nuts and seeds, herbs and spices—combined with beans and grains—offers ample inspiration for outstanding gourmet vegan meals. In these pages, we unleash the seasoning potential of fresh ginger and garlic, mustards, flavored oils and vinegars, capers and olives, chili peppers, and the like to make these simple, healthful foods taste extraordinary.

This volume contains some of the favorite vegan dishes from our BEST 125 MEATLESS cookbook series, plus many exciting new dishes. We went to work in our kitchens and invited friends to the table to prove that vegan cooking can transcend its humble reputation. Our delicious inventions include main dishes such as Porcini Mushroom Stroganoff and Curried Lentil Stir-Fry with Fennel and Apricots, as well as creative accompaniments such as Sweet Red Pepper Strips with Artichoke and Caper Filling. We believe the resulting collection will entice both beginning and experienced vegan cooks.

To help make busy lives easier, a good number of these recipes are "Almost Instant," requiring 30 minutes or less to prepare. The novice may want to follow the suggestions provided with many recipes for rounding out the meal. In addition, menu plans for special occasion, multicourse feasts are distributed throughout the book.

As in all our books, nutritional data is provided for each recipe. This allows careful monitoring of calories, protein, carbohydrates, sodium, cholesterol, and fat consumption by those concerned with such matters. Since dietary cholesterol is derived only from animal products, the recipes in this book are all cholesterol-free.

Now we invite you into our kitchens to share in the discovery that vegan cooking can be infinitely pleasurable.

A Note on the Revised Edition

Though natural health systems emphasizing proper diet have flourished throughout the world for centuries, modern science is only now discovering the hows and whys of the diet–health connection. Every month, scientists release the results of new research that demonstrates how certain substances in foods can either heal or hurt us. In this golden age of nutrition, we can profoundly improve the quality of our lives—perhaps even the quantity of our years—by making more intelligent food choices based on what we learn from the research.

But to find one's optimum health-promoting diet is not necessarily an easy task. No single diet is right for every body. Almost every nutrition program is helpful for some who follow it; a few programs appear to benefit large numbers of people. Only we can know for sure what works for us. When a certain way of eating, applied consistently over a period of months, provides us with strong and dependable energy, freedom from disease and allergic reactions, glowing hair and skin, smoothly functioning digestion and elimination, and a sense of general well-being—only then can we know that it is a good diet for us.

Many people today choose the vegan path (usually pronounced vee-gun), and completely eliminate animal products from their diets. The vegan diet is free of cholesterol, low in saturated fat, and high in fiber and complex carbohydrates. Protein intake is moderate but quite sufficient if a good quantity and variety of legumes and whole grains are eaten on a regular basis. The vegan way of eating is kind to our bodies, to animals, and to the earth. What's more, it's economical: Eliminating meat and dairy products from the daily diet would slash the grocery budget for most families in America.

You can discover for yourself the positive effects of the vegan diet by putting aside animal foods for a few weeks. During this trial, be sure to eat a diversity of plant foods from high-quality sources. When beginning the regimen, note any health complaints (for example, headaches or digestion troubles), then keep a diary of your body's well-being while eating the vegan way. At the end of a month, you may understand what makes this way of eating an increasingly popular one. You will probably feel lighter, less fatigued, and cleaner from the inside out more than usual. Your energy level is likely to be more stable and your moods may even improve.

Far from limiting food options, a move away from meat opens up a world of new foods and flavors for most people. The shelves and bins of any natural-food store provide ample inspiration for vegan cooking. Most importantly, an attitude of adventure and a commitment to good health can guide you well in exploring the potential of the vegan path for you and your loved ones.

We offer this updated edition of *The Vegan Gourmet* with gratitude to our faithful readers. May you be well.

RECOMMENDED MENUS

APPETIZERS

* * * * * * * *

APPETIZERS

Sweet Red Pepper Strips with Artichoke and Caper Filling

Marinated Tofu Skewers with Cherry Tomatoes

Mushrooms Stuffed with Spinach, Bread Crumbs,
and Fresh Herbs

Red Lentil Pâté with Tarragon

Olive, Basil, and Walnut Spread with Madeira

Mushroom Tempeh Pâté with Sage

Black Bean Puree with Fresh Guacamole

Marinated Garbanzos, Zucchini, and Olives

Focaccia with Fresh Rosemary and Sautéed Onions

Cannellini Beans in Mint Marinade

Crostini with Greek Eggplant Topping

Spiced Carrot Spread

P EOPLE LOVE TO NIBBLE, so whenever friends or family gather, appetizers are a welcome treat. They can be casual or fancy—eaten with the fingers or a fork, standing up or sitting down. Served singly, they awaken our appetites and make us eager for the dishes that will follow; served in sumptuous abundance, they become a tantalizing buffet meal.

Many appetizers are quick to prepare or can be made well in advance. This leaves time to get creative with presentation by using pretty plates and bowls, rustic baskets, edible flowers, and elaborate cut garnishes. Approach this task like an artist, relishing the interplay of colors, shapes, and textures. Set the appetizers out where you want people to gather, then mingle awhile with your guests before going back to the kitchen, enjoying the celebratory mood the beautiful food helps to foster.

Beyond cheese and crackers or chips and dips, there is a world of appetizers to explore and enjoy. We present a few of our favorites in this chapter.

Sweet Red Pepper Strips with Artichoke and Caper Filling

ALMOST INSTANT

Here is an elegant appetizer suitable for any dinner party. You may make up the artichoke mixture several hours ahead of time and hold it at room temperature, then cut and fill the pepper strips just before your guests arrive. Be sure to mince the artichokes, onion, and parsley very finely for best results.

YIELD: 6 APPETIZER SERVINGS

1 can (13¾-ounce) water-packed artichoke bottoms
⅓ cup minced red onion
2 tablespoons capers, drained, minced if large
¼ cup minced fresh parsley leaves
1 tablespoon Dijon mustard
1 tablespoon extra-virgin olive oil
2 tablespoons apple cider vinegar
1 teaspoon dried basil, crushed
1 teaspoon sweet paprika
Several grinds black pepper
2 medium red bell peppers

DRAIN the artichoke bottoms and mince them finely. Toss with the onion, capers, and parsley. Stir together the mustard, olive oil, vinegar, basil, paprika, and black pepper. Toss with the artichoke mixture until well combined. Set aside. Cut the bell peppers in half lengthwise. Discard the stems, seeds, and white membranes and cut each half pepper into 3 lengthwise strips, taking care to create strips with a cupped shape that can hold the filling. Spoon the artichoke mixture along the length of each bell pepper strip. Arrange the filled pepper strips in a pretty pattern on a serving dish. Serve at room temperature.

EACH SERVING PROVIDES:

57 calories, 2g protein, 3g fat, 2g dietary fiber

8g carbohydrate, 364mg sodium, 0mg cholesterol

ITALIAN BUFFET SUPPER

Sweet Red Pepper Strips with Artichoke
and Caper Filling, page 4

Cannellini Beans in Mint Marinade, page 21

Spicy Eggplant Pasta Salad with
Calamata Olives, page 38

Focaccia with Fresh Rosemary and
Sautéed Onions, page 18

A selection of pepperoncini and gourmet olives

Italian Pinot Grigio or California Sauvignon Blanc

Marinated Tofu Skewers with Cherry Tomatoes

This recipe makes a festive appetizer; plan on one or two skewers per person. It can also be a showy main dish if you serve three skewers per person.

YIELD: 12 SKEWERS

14 ounces firm tofu
2 tablespoons fresh-squeezed lime juice
1 tablespoon dark sesame oil
1 tablespoon soy sauce
1 teaspoon minced fresh ginger
½ teaspoon granulated garlic
½ teaspoon Chinese five-spice powder
¾ pound cherry tomatoes

12 wooden skewers

PAT the tofu dry and cut it into 1-inch cubes. Prepare the marinade in a medium bowl by whisking together the lime juice, oil, soy sauce, ginger, garlic, and Chinese five-spice powder. Place the tofu in a 2-quart glass baking dish and drizzle with the marinade. Allow to marinate for about 1 hour, turning gently with a spatula after about 30 minutes.

Preheat the oven to 350 degrees F. and bake the tofu, uncovered, for 25 minutes, turning it gently midway through the cooking time so the liquid coats and evaporates evenly. Remove from the oven and allow to cool slightly.

Place 3 cubes of tofu separated by 2 tomatoes on each skewer. Arrange on a platter and serve at room temperature.

EACH SERVING PROVIDES:

46 calories, 2.3g protein, 3.5g fat, 0.4g dietary fiber

2.1g carbohydrate, 85mg sodium, 0mg cholesterol

CHINESE FIVE-SPICE

This assertive blend of exotic seasonings is delicious when paired with tofu, rice, or mixed vegetables. It is also delightful as a seasoning for spice cakes, cookies, quick breads, and fruit salads. Purchase a commercially made blend, or combine equal amounts of the following ground spices: anise, fennel, licorice root, ginger, cinnamon, and cloves. Stir together and store in an airtight jar.

Mushrooms Stuffed with Spinach, Bread Crumbs, and Fresh Herbs

These succulent morsels make a delectable appetizer. This recipe was tested using mushrooms that were about 2 inches in diameter; you may substitute a larger quantity of smaller mushrooms, but they must be large enough to have a fairly flat cap so they can sit securely on a plate. If you do not have access to fresh herbs, substitute 1 teaspoon each dried rosemary and basil.

YIELD: 6 APPETIZER SERVINGS

¾ pound fresh spinach (about 1 bunch)
12 large button mushrooms (about 1 pound)
1 tablespoon olive oil
2 tablespoons minced white onion
1 clove garlic, minced
1 tablespoon minced fresh basil leaves
1 tablespoon minced fresh rosemary leaves
Pinch plus ⅛ teaspoon salt
1¼ cups Homemade Vegetable Stock (see NOTE)
½ cup coarse dry bread crumbs
2 tablespoons dry sherry
1 teaspoon balsamic vinegar
Several grinds black pepper

CAREFULLY wash the spinach and discard the stems. Without drying them, pile the leaves into a stockpot. Cover and cook over medium heat 5 minutes, or until the spinach wilts. Transfer to a colander to drain. When the spinach is cool enough to handle, chop it very finely and set aside in a medium mixing bowl.

Remove the stems from the mushrooms, keeping the caps intact. Mince the stems. Heat the oil in a small sauté pan over medium heat. Add the mushroom stems, onion, garlic, basil, rosemary, and the pinch of salt. Stir and sauté for 3–4 minutes, until the stems have softened and released some of their liquid. Add ¼ cup of the stock and quickly stir and cook for 2–3 minutes longer, until only about 2 tablespoons of liquid remain. Scrape the contents of the pan into the bowl that holds the spinach. Add the bread crumbs, sherry, vinegar, the ⅛ teaspoon salt, and pepper. Stir until well combined. If the mixture is too dry, add water, a tablespoon at a time, to create a stuffing mixture that holds together. You don't want a crumbly texture.

Preheat the broiler. Place the mushroom caps hollow side up in a single layer in a broad skillet. Add the remaining 1 cup stock, cover the pan, and steam over medium-high heat about 5 minutes. Turn the mushrooms over, replace the cover, and steam an additional 2–3 minutes, until mushrooms are just tender but not shriveled. Place the mushrooms on a clean tea towel to drain for a moment. (Refrigerate the steaming liquid for another use, such as soup stock, if you wish.)

When the mushroom caps are cool enough to handle, stuff each one with filling, shaping it into a smooth, heaping mound. Transfer the stuffed mushrooms to a broiler pan or ovenproof dish and place under the preheated broiler for 3–5 minutes, until nicely browned. Watch closely so they do not burn. Dust lightly with paprika, if you wish. Serve warm or at room temperature.

NOTE: If you do not have Homemade Vegetable Stock on hand, make some according to the directions on page 84, or dissolve ½ of a large low-sodium vegetable broth cube in 1¼ cups of hot water.

EACH SERVING PROVIDES:
94 calories, 4g protein, 3g fat, 2g dietary fiber
13g carbohydrate, 214mg sodium, 0mg cholesterol

Red Lentil Pâté with Tarragon

We like to serve this lovely, aromatic pâté with a whole grain baguette or other crusty bread. It is also delicious served with crackers and assorted vegetables.

YIELD: 12 APPETIZER SERVINGS

1 cup dried red lentils
1 small yellow onion, chopped
2 bay leaves
5 cloves garlic
¼ cup fresh-squeezed lemon juice
3 tablespoons extra-virgin olive oil
2 teaspoons dried tarragon
½ teaspoon salt
Several grinds black pepper

SORT and rinse the lentils, discarding any foreign objects. Bring 4 cups of water to a boil and add the lentils, onion, and bay leaves. Reduce the heat to medium-high and cook for about 10 minutes, until tender. Meanwhile, place the garlic in a food processor and pulse to mince.

Discard the bay leaves. Drain the lentils and onions and transfer them to the food processor. Add the lemon juice, oil, tarragon, salt, and pepper. Puree until smooth. Transfer to ramekins or a pretty serving dish, cover, and refrigerate about an hour before serving. Any leftovers can be refrigerated for several days, but return to room temperature before serving.

EACH SERVING PROVIDES:
88 calories, 4g protein, 4g fat, 2g dietary fiber
11g carbohydrate, 91mg sodium, 0mg cholesterol

Olive, Basil, and Walnut Spread with Madeira

ALMOST INSTANT

The sharp flavor of pimiento-stuffed olives is mellowed here by the other ingredients, creating a tantalizing pesto-like spread. It can launch any Greek or Italian menu with real gusto. If you decide to serve it with crackers, choose some that are plain and simple so they don't compete with the flavor of the spread.

YIELD: 12 APPETIZER SERVINGS

1 cup pimiento-stuffed green olives, drained
⅔ cup chopped fresh basil leaves
½ cup chopped raw walnuts
¼ cup Madeira
1 tablespoon fresh-squeezed lemon juice
2 cloves garlic, chopped
Several grinds black pepper

PUREE all the ingredients in a food processor until thick and fairly homogenous. Prepare the spread well ahead of time, if possible, so the flavors have time to blend. Cover the mixture and store in the refrigerator for up to a week, but return to room temperature before serving. Serve in a pretty bowl, with fresh baguette slices or crisp, simple crackers in a basket on the side.

EACH SERVING PROVIDES:

37 calories, 1g protein, 3g fat, 1g dietary fiber
2g carbohydrate, 271mg sodium, 0mg cholesterol

Mushroom Tempeh Pâté with Sage

Tempeh is available at all natural food stores and in some well-stocked supermarkets. It is produced from whole soybeans that have been fermented, creating a delicious nutty flavor. This pâté travels well, so we prepare it often as part of a picnic lunch. Enjoy it on a sunny spring day with a good baguette, fresh fruit, and Sonoma Chardonnay.

YIELD: 10 APPETIZER SERVINGS

¼ pound button mushrooms
2 tablespoons olive oil
4 ounces tempeh, cubed
1 cup chopped red onion
2 cloves garlic, minced
3 tablespoons dry sherry
1 tablespoon low-sodium soy sauce
1 teaspoon rubbed sage
⅛ teaspoon ground allspice

BRUSH or wipe the mushrooms clean and chop them coarsely. Heat the oil in a medium skillet over medium-high heat and add the tempeh, mushrooms, onion, and garlic. Cook, stirring frequently, for 10 minutes. The mushroom liquid will evaporate and the mushrooms and onions will brown slightly. Stir in the sherry, soy sauce, sage, and allspice. Cook, stirring constantly, about 5 minutes, until the liquid is gone. Remove from the heat and allow to cool.

Puree the mixture in a food processor to a thick, homogenous consistency. Spoon into a serving bowl, cover, and refrigerate for at least 1 hour, or up to 3 days. Serve at room temperature with crisp crackers or baguette slices.

EACH SERVING PROVIDES:

51 calories, 3g protein, 2g fat, 1g dietary fiber
4g carbohydrate, 63mg sodium, 0mg cholesterol

A CLASSIC FIRST COURSE

Here is an elegant way to begin a formal dinner party. Place a small ramekin filled with pâté on a lettuce leaf. Garnish the pâté with whole fresh sage leaves and finish the plate with yellow or red bell pepper strips, a few cornichons, and baguette slices. Set out one plate for each guest.

Black Bean Puree with Fresh Guacamole

ALMOST INSTANT

This puree is lovely enough for a Southwest dinner party and so delicious your family will request it often. Present it in a bright red or yellow shallow bowl for a real visual treat, with a few sprigs of cilantro, minced onion, and a dusting of red chili powder for garnish. Serve the bean puree with tortilla chips and raw jicama and bell pepper strips.

YIELD: 8 APPETIZER SERVINGS

1 small serrano chile
2 cups freshly cooked or canned black beans, drained
2 tablespoons tomato juice
2 tablespoons fresh-squeezed lime juice
1 small clove garlic, chopped
1 teaspoon dried oregano
¼ teaspoon plus pinch salt
1 medium ripe avocado
2 tablespoons grated white onion
2 tablespoons minced cilantro leaves
1 teaspoon fresh-squeezed lemon juice
Several grinds black pepper

REMOVE and discard the stem of the chile. Cut the chile in half lengthwise and scrape out the seeds, if you wish. Leaving the seeds in will increase the heat of the dish. Coarsely chop the chile.

In a food processor, combine the beans, tomato juice, lime juice, garlic, oregano, and the ¼ teaspoon salt with the chile. Puree to a fairly smooth consistency. At this point, the puree can be refrigerated in a covered container for up to a few days.

Just before serving, place the puree in a pretty, shallow serving bowl, smoothing out the top with a rubber spatula. Peel the avocado and discard the seed. In a bowl, mash the avocado with the onion, cilantro, lemon juice, the pinch of salt, and pepper until fairly smooth. Spread the avocado mixture over the black beans, leaving a 1-inch border of beans showing. Garnish as described in the recipe introduction, and serve immediately.

EACH SERVING PROVIDES:

103 calories, 5g protein, 4g fat, 3g dietary fiber
13g carbohydrate, 106mg sodium, 0mg cholesterol

Marinated Garbanzos, Zucchini, and Olives

ALMOST INSTANT

This marinated salad makes a wonderful antipasto course for any Italian-inspired meal. Serve it with crusty country bread and fruity red wine. Select flavorful olives for best results, such as gaeta or calamata. There is no need to pit the olives—this is a rustic dish, after all—but warn your diners that the olives have pits.

YIELD: 8 APPETIZER SERVINGS

¾ pound zucchini (about 2 medium)
½ medium red onion
2½ cups freshly cooked or canned garbanzo beans, drained
½ cup unpitted gaeta, calamata, or other exotic olives
¼ cup minced fresh parsley leaves
2 tablespoons extra-virgin olive oil
4 tablespoons fresh-squeezed lemon juice
¼ teaspoon salt
Several grinds black pepper

TRIM off and discard the stem and flower ends of the zucchini. Cut the zucchini in half lengthwise. Cut the halves crosswise into ½-inch slices. Steam or parboil for a few minutes until barely fork-tender. Rinse briefly under cold water. Coarsely dice or slice the onion.

In a serving bowl, toss together the beans, zucchini, onion, olives, and parsley. Drizzle the oil over the mixture and toss to combine. Add the lemon juice, salt, and plenty of pepper. Toss again.

Taste the mixture and add more lemon juice, salt, or pepper, if desired. Serve immediately or refrigerate for a few hours, but return to room temperature before serving.

EACH SERVING PROVIDES:

147 calories, 5g protein, 7g fat, 3g dietary fiber

18g carbohydrate, 337mg sodium, 0mg cholesterol

MARINATED BEANS

A marinated bean and vegetable medley is a wonderful make-ahead appetizer. A day or two in the refrigerator may even improve its flavor, but return the mixture to room temperature before serving.

Focaccia with Fresh Rosemary and Sautéed Onions

This focaccia is rich with the earthy flavor of rosemary and the sweetness of sautéed red onions. It makes a terrific snack alone or a scrumptious addition to an antipasti table. Pack it with a chunky vegetable salad and a light red wine for a fine picnic feast.

YIELD: 12 APPETIZER SERVINGS (24 3-INCH SQUARES)

The dough
¼ ounce active dry yeast (1 envelope)
1½ cups lukewarm water (105–115 degrees F.)
3 tablespoons plus ½ teaspoon extra-virgin olive oil
½ teaspoon salt
3½ to 4 cups unbleached flour
¼ cup minced fresh rosemary leaves

The focaccia
4 tablespoons extra-virgin olive oil
2 pounds red onions, thinly sliced
1½ teaspoons coarse sea salt
½ cup fresh rosemary sprigs, about 1 inch in length

To make the dough, place the yeast in a large bowl and add the warm water. Stir with a wooden spoon to dissolve the yeast, then set aside in a warm place until creamy in appearance, about 15 minutes. Stir in 2 tablespoons of the oil and the salt, then add

2 cups of the flour and the minced rosemary. Stir to incorporate, using a large wooden spoon. The mixture will be very sticky at this point. Add 1 more cup of the flour and continue to stir until the dough begins to form a ball. Turn out onto a lightly floured work surface and knead the dough until it is soft and smooth, about 10 minutes, adding the remaining flour as needed, a bit at a time, until the dough is no longer sticky. Too much flour will result in a dry dough that can become a slightly tough crust, so don't add any more flour than necessary.

Rub a large bowl with the ½ teaspoon of oil. Place the dough ball in the oiled bowl, turn it to coat the entire surface with oil, and cover the bowl with a clean tea towel. Place the bowl in a warm, draft-free place for the dough to rise until doubled in volume, about 1½ hours. (An unlit oven or warm cupboard works well.) After it has risen, punch the dough down with your fist or fingertips to press out most of the air.

Transfer the dough to a lightly floured work surface and slap it down firmly a few times. Place 1 tablespoon of the oil in a lipped 12 × 18-inch baking sheet. Distribute the oil evenly over the bottom and sides of the sheet. Place the dough in the center, and, pressing with your hands from the middle of the dough, carefully stretch it until it covers the sheet completely in an even layer. Cover with a damp cloth and set aside to rise again for 45 minutes.

While the dough is rising for the second time, heat 2 tablespoons of the oil over medium heat. Add the onions and toss with tongs to distribute the oil. Sauté for 12–15 minutes, tossing occasionally, until onions are soft and almost all their liquid has evaporated.

(continued)

(Fococcia with Fresh Rosemary and Sautéed Onions, *continued*)

Preheat the oven to 425 degrees F. When the dough has finished rising for the second time, use your fingertips to gently dimple the surface of the dough with shallow indentations. Coat the top with 2 tablespoons of the oil and dust evenly with the salt. Distribute the onions evenly over the dough and bake 25 minutes. Remove from the oven and distribute the rosemary sprigs evenly over the bread. Bake 5–7 minutes longer, until the bottom of the bread is lightly browned (use a spatula to lift the bread gently to check for browning).

Cut into 3-inch squares and serve hot or at room temperature.

EACH SERVING PROVIDES:
257 calories, 5g protein, 9g fat, 3g dietary fiber
39g carbohydrate, 356mg sodium, 0mg cholesterol

Cannellini Beans in Mint Marinade

The mint is a delightful, fresh surprise in this marinade. On the island of Sicily and in Southern Italy, fresh mint is used as a primary herbal seasoning. These beans are a wonderful antipasto by themselves or a tasty addition to an antipasti platter. You might also enjoy them served on butter lettuce leaves as a side dish.

YIELD: 10 APPETIZER SERVINGS

⅓ cup extra-virgin olive oil
¼ cup fresh-squeezed lemon juice
¼ teaspoon salt
Several grinds black pepper
¼ cup minced fresh mint leaves
3½ cups freshly cooked or canned cannellini beans, drained

WHISK together the oil, lemon juice, salt, and pepper in a medium-size bowl. Stir in the mint. Add the beans to the marinade. Gently toss to coat, then allow them to marinate at room temperature for several hours before serving. Any leftovers may be refrigerated but should be returned to room temperature before serving.

EACH SERVING PROVIDES:
152 calories, 6g protein, 7g fat, 3g dietary fiber
16g carbohydrate, 48mg sodium, 0mg cholesterol

Crostini with Greek Eggplant Topping

Eggplant combines very well with the classic flavors of the Mediterranean, as demonstrated in this recipe. Any leftover eggplant topping can be stored in a tightly closed container in the refrigerator and enjoyed over the course of a few days. Leftover crostini will retain their crispness for a day or two if stored at room temperature in a tightly closed plastic bag.

YIELD: 12 APPETIZER SERVINGS

2 pounds eggplant (2 medium)
¼ cup diced white onion
2 cloves garlic, minced
¼ cup minced fresh parsley leaves
1 tablespoon minced fresh oregano leaves
3 tablespoons fresh-squeezed lemon juice
⅓ cup extra-virgin olive oil
1 loaf (1 pound) fresh thick-crusted bread

PREHEAT the oven to 400 degrees F. Do not peel the eggplants, but pierce them in several places with a fork. Place the whole eggplants in an ovenproof glass dish. Bake for 40–50 minutes, until very soft. The skin will scorch slightly. Remove eggplants from the oven and set aside to cool. When they are cool enough to handle, cut in half lengthwise and scrape the pulp from the skin. Discard any dense pockets of dark seeds.

Place the eggplant pulp in a food processor and pulse to coarsely chop; do not puree. Drain off any liquid that may separate from the pulp. Add the onion, garlic, parsley, and oregano and pulse to combine. With the machine running, add the lemon juice and then the oil in a thin stream. Don't overprocess—the resulting mixture should be a thick, slightly chunky puree. Transfer to a serving bowl and chill for several hours.

Shortly before serving time, make the crostini. Preheat a broiler or a coal or gas grill to medium. If the bread has a long, skinny shape (like a baguette), cut it across its width into ½-inch slices. If you are using a dome-shaped loaf, cut it in half from top to bottom, then cut each half crosswise into ½-inch slices. Arrange the slices in a single layer on the broiler pan or directly on the grill. Cook about 2 minutes per side, until the bread is lightly browned and crisp on the outside, but still soft and chewy on the inside. Don't toast the bread for too long or it will dry out completely.

Stack the crostini on a serving plate and serve it with the eggplant topping on the side.

EACH SERVING PROVIDES:

180 calories, 4g protein, 7g fat, 2g dietary fiber

24g carbohydrate, 222mg sodium, 0mg cholesterol

Spiced Carrot Spread

ALMOST INSTANT

The lovely color and tantalizing flavor of this spread make it an often requested appetizer. Serve with toasted baguette slices or crisp sesame crackers.

YIELD: 12 APPETIZER SERVINGS

1 pound carrots
½ pound russet potato (1 medium)
2 cups fresh bread cubes, crust removed
2 tablespoons extra-virgin olive oil
2 tablespoons fresh-squeezed lemon juice
2 medium cloves garlic, minced
2 teaspoons ground cumin
2 teaspoons paprika
1 teaspoon ground coriander
¼ teaspoon salt
⅛ teaspoon cayenne

SCRUB the carrots and dice them. Peel the potato and dice it. Place the carrots and potatoes in the saucepan with enough water to submerge them and bring to a boil. Cook for 10–15 minutes, until very tender.

Drain well and transfer half the mixture to a food processor. Add the bread, oil, lemon juice, garlic, cumin, paprika, coriander, salt, and cayenne and process until the bread is smoothly incorporated. Add the remaining carrots and potatoes and pulse until finely chopped.

Serve at room temperature or chill before serving. May be refrigerated, covered, for up to two days before serving. Garnish with mint or parsley leaves, if available.

EACH SERVING PROVIDES:

99 calories, 2.5g protein, 2.6g fat, 1.1g dietary fiber
16.8g carbohydrate, 158mg sodium, 1mg cholesterol

SALADS

• • • • • • • •

• • • • • • • •

SALADS

Artichokes Stuffed with Marinated French Lentils

Spinach, Kiwi, and Grapefruit Salad with Cilantro
Sherry Vinaigrette

Mixed Greens with Peas and Mustard
Miso Vinaigrette

Green Beans with Watercress and Orange Mint Vinaigrette

Spicy Eggplant Pasta Salad with Calamata Olives

Couscous Salad with Dried Tomato Vinaigrette

Bulgur with Tomatoes, Mint, and Toasted Pine Nuts

Rice and Lentil Salad with Pimiento-Stuffed Olives

Black-Eyed Peas, Corn, and Toasted Walnuts with
Spicy/Sweet Vinaigrette

Sweet Potatoes, Wheat Berries, and Peppers with
Tomato Chive Vinaigrette

Mushroom, Radish, and Celery Salad with Lemon
and Garlic

Potatoes and Artichokes with Mustard Caper Vinaigrette

Golden Beet, Jicama, and Cucumber Salad with Fresh Mint

S ALAD-MAKING IS A KIND OF ARTISTRY, directed by the seasons. When temperatures soar, nothing is more appetizing than a cool, brimming bowl of brightly colored vegetables, lightly dressed to summery perfection. Brilliant red garden tomatoes and multi-colored peppers are irresistible. In cold weather, hearty combinations of grains, beans, and cooked vegetables provide satisfying nourishment. We are captivated by winter radishes, red cabbage, and the emerald green of baby spinach. Whatever the season, the treasures of the garden provide endless inspiration.

Good salads depend upon inspired dressings. We keep our pantries well stocked with a variety of vinegars, fla-vorful oils, and fresh and dried herbs, drawing upon a wide variety of seasonings to create tantalizing salads.

As the recipes in this chapter demonstrate, salads never need become mundane and boring.

Artichokes Stuffed with Marinated French Lentils

This beautifully composed salad features the small, dark green French Le Puy lentils. They have a slightly peppery flavor and are smaller in size and more dense in texture than the more common brown lentil. The roasted red bell peppers called for may be commercially prepared. Serve this dish as the first course at your next dinner party.

YIELD: 4 SIDE-DISH SERVINGS

½ cup dried green lentils
2 bay leaves
1 tablespoon minced white onion

The marinade
3 tablespoons extra-virgin olive oil
1 tablespoon balsamic vinegar
2 cloves garlic, minced
Pinch dried red chili flakes
2 teaspoons dried tarragon
¼ cup chopped roasted red bell pepper

The artichokes
2 tablespoons fresh-squeezed lemon juice
1 teaspoon olive oil
1 teaspoon dried tarragon
2 cloves garlic
2 large artichokes

SORT and rinse the lentils, discarding any foreign objects. Bring 2 cups of water to a boil along with the bay leaves and onion. Add the lentils and return to a boil. Reduce heat to medium-low and simmer for about 20 minutes, until the lentils are just tender. Be sure not to overcook the lentils, as you want a firm texture. Drain the lentils into a colander, gently shaking to remove the water, then transfer to a bowl. Remove the bay leaves.

Meanwhile, make the marinade by whisking together the olive oil, balsamic vinegar, garlic, chili flakes, and tarragon. Pour the marinade over the lentils, add the red bell pepper, and toss gently to combine. Set aside at room temperature to marinate while you prepare the artichokes.

In a large, wide-bottomed saucepan, combine 2 cups of water with the lemon juice, olive oil, tarragon, and garlic. Trim only about ¼ inch from the stem end of each artichoke, then peel the stems. Trim the pointed ends off the artichoke leaves and cut the artichokes in half lengthwise. Use a paring knife or melon baller to remove the fuzzy "choke" portion from each half, placing each half into the saucepan while you prepare the next. Cover the pan and bring to a rapid simmer over high heat. Reduce heat to medium and continue to cook for about 30 minutes, until just fork-tender. Remove from the heat, drain, and place on individual serving plates.

Allow the artichokes to cool, then spoon equal amounts of the marinated lentils into each cavity, allowing some to spill onto the plate. Serve warm or at room temperature.

EACH SERVING PROVIDES:
212 calories, 9g protein, 11g fat, 7g dietary fiber
24g carbohydrate, 196mg sodium, 0mg cholesterol

Spinach, Kiwi, and Grapefruit Salad with Cilantro Sherry Vinaigrette

This composed salad is light, refreshing, and stunning on the plate. If you have calendulas in your garden, pick one and scatter the edible petals over each salad. Kiwis are often hard when purchased, and are not sweet and ready to eat until they soften up enough to yield to light pressure. Purchase them a few days ahead of time, if necessary, and allow them to ripen in a basket in your kitchen.

YIELD: 4 SIDE-DISH SERVINGS

2 tablespoons fresh-squeezed orange juice
1 tablespoon olive oil
2 teaspoons sherry vinegar
¼ teaspoon Dijon mustard
Pinch salt
2 teaspoons grated red onion
1 heaping teaspoon minced fresh cilantro leaves
6 ounces fresh spinach (about ½ bunch)
1 medium pink grapefruit, chilled
2 medium kiwis, chilled

In a small bowl, whisk together the orange juice, olive oil, vinegar, mustard, and salt until well combined and creamy. Stir in the red onion and cilantro and set aside at room temperature.

Carefully wash the spinach, discarding the stems. Dry thoroughly and set aside in the refrigerator. Peel the grapefruit and divide it into individual sections. Remove and discard the membrane from each section, discard any seeds, and break the fruit into bite-size pieces. Set aside in the refrigerator. Peel the kiwis and cut crosswise into thin slices.

Arrange a bed of spinach on each of 4 chilled salad plates. Artfully arrange portions of grapefruit and kiwi on top of the spinach. Drizzle each salad with dressing and garnish with calendula petals, if available.

EACH SERVING PROVIDES:

83 calories, 2g protein, 4g fat, 2g dietary fiber

12g carbohydrate, 69mg sodium, 0mg cholesterol

Mixed Greens with Peas and Mustard Miso Vinaigrette

ALMOST INSTANT

Here is a wonderful lowfat salad dressing that also can be called into service as a light sauce for hot vegetables or grains. Use your favorite greens from the garden for this salad or the "mixed greens" available in many supermarkets. You may add leftover cooked grains or beans to the bowl, if you wish. If you are using fresh peas, you will need to purchase about one pound of plump English pea pods, which will yield about one cup of shelled peas.

YIELD: 6 SIDE-DISH SERVINGS

$\frac{1}{4}$ cup light-colored miso
3 tablespoons whole grain mustard
2 tablespoons apple cider vinegar
1 tablespoon mirin or sweet sherry
1 cup fresh or frozen shelled peas
6 cups torn mixed salad greens
1 cup finely shredded red cabbage

IN a small bowl, whisk together the miso, mustard, vinegar, mirin, and 3 tablespoons of water. Set aside so the flavors can blend. Bring 1 cup of water to a boil in a small saucepan. Add the peas and cook for 2 minutes if using frozen peas, 4–5 minutes if fresh. Rinse the peas under cold water to stop the cooking and drain well.

In a serving bowl, toss together the greens, cabbage, and peas, then add the dressing and toss again. Serve immediately.

EACH SERVING PROVIDES:

77 calories, 4g protein, 2g fat, 2g dietary fiber

11g carbohydrate, 502mg sodium, 0mg cholesterol

NO·OIL SALAD DRESSINGS

Tomato and citrus juices, seasoned vinegars, and gourmet mustards are flavorful foundations upon which to build delicious no-oil salad dressings. Experiment with different combinations of these liquid bases, whisked together with your choice of fresh and dried herbs, garlic, capers, miso or soy sauce, salt, and pepper. You are sure to invent some wonderful dressings that will become family favorites.

Green Beans with Watercress and Orange Mint Vinaigrette

ALMOST INSTANT

A study in green, this salad is refreshingly light in flavor, yet full-bodied and satisfying. If you can't find peppery watercress at your local markets substitute fresh spinach for a different but still quite delicious salad. Nasturtium blossoms, if available, make a lovely garnish.

YIELD: 6 SIDE-DISH SERVINGS

¾ pound fresh green beans (preferably Blue Lake or
    Chinese long)
2 tablespoons hulled sunflower seeds
2 tablespoons olive oil
2 tablespoons cider vinegar
¼ cup fresh-squeezed orange juice
½ teaspoon grated orange peel
¼ teaspoon salt
Several grinds black pepper
2 cups chopped watercress
¼ cup minced red onion
¼ cup fresh mint leaves, chiffonade (see NOTE)

WASH the beans, string them if necessary, and cut into 2-inch pieces. Place the beans on a steamer rack in a saucepan that has a tight-fitting lid. Add about 1 inch water, cover the pan, and cook over medium-high heat until barely tender, about 7 minutes. Plunge the beans into ice water to set the color, then drain well.

Meanwhile, toast the sunflower seeds in a heavy skillet over medium-high heat, stirring almost constantly until they darken in color a shade or two and emit a toasted aroma. Remove the seeds from the pan and set aside.

To prepare the dressing, whisk together the oil, vinegar, orange juice, orange peel, salt, and pepper. Toss the beans, watercress, and onion in a bowl. Pour in the dressing; toss gently. Transfer to a serving dish and garnish with the sunflower seeds.

NOTE: To cut fresh herbs chiffonade style, stack several clean and dried leaves, roll tightly from one long side to the other, and slice crosswise as thinly as possible with a sharp knife.

EACH SERVING PROVIDES:
85 calories, 2.2g protein, 6.1g fat, 2.5g dietary fiber
7g carbohydrate, 99mg sodium, 0mg cholesterol

Spicy Eggplant Pasta Salad with Calamata Olives

We find the balance of sweet, sour, and spicy just right in this distinctive salad. We set out to duplicate a dish we had enjoyed at a gourmet lunch counter in Berkeley. Our own ideas took over and it turned out not the same at all, though just as delicious. This dish is interesting and rich enough to carry a meal as a main course.

YIELD: 8 MAIN-DISH SERVINGS

2 small eggplants (about 1½ pounds)
7 green onions
3 tablespoons extra-virgin olive oil
4 medium cloves garlic, minced
1 teaspoon dried red chili flakes
1 medium red bell pepper, thinly sliced
2 teaspoons dried oregano
½ teaspoon salt
¼ cup fresh-squeezed lemon juice
2 tablespoons balsamic vinegar
2 tablespoons mirin
1 pound dried rigatoni
½ cup slivered calamata olives
½ cup minced fresh parsley

PEEL the eggplants and cut them into ¼-inch-thick strips about 3 inches in length. Trim all but about 2 inches of the tops from the green onions. Cut in half lengthwise, then into 1-inch pieces.

Heat 2 tablespoons of the olive oil in a heavy skillet over medium heat. Add the garlic and chili flakes and stir to distribute in the oil. Add the eggplant, green onion, and bell pepper; stir. Sprinkle with the oregano and ¼ teaspoon of the salt. Stir and sauté over medium heat 15–20 minutes, until vegetables are tender and browning nicely. Transfer to a bowl.

Whisk together the remaining 1 tablespoon olive oil, the lemon juice, vinegar, mirin, and remaining ¼ teaspoon salt. Pour this dressing over the eggplant mixture in the bowl, cover, and set aside at room temperature for at least 30 minutes or up to a few hours so the flavors can blend.

Bring several quarts of water to a boil. Cook the pasta until al dente. Cool briefly in a bowl of cold water, drain very well, and toss with the eggplant mixture, olives, and parsley.

EACH SERVING PROVIDES:

338 calories, 8g protein, 12g fat, 5g dietary fiber

50g carbohydrate, 429mg sodium, 0mg cholesterol

Couscous Salad with Dried Tomato Vinaigrette

Though this salad has many steps, it is not difficult to prepare. The balance of sweet, smoky, and spicy is delicious.

YIELD: 6 SIDE-DISH SERVINGS

The dressing

⅓ cup minced dried tomato (see NOTE)

¼ cup olive oil

3 tablespoons red wine vinegar

1 teaspoon dried oregano

¼ teaspoon salt

⅛ teaspoon cayenne

1 tablespoon mustard seeds

1 tablespoon cumin seeds

⅓ cup minced fresh cilantro leaves

The salad

1 medium red bell pepper

2 cups dried couscous

¼ teaspoon salt

¼ teaspoon granulated garlic

1 medium cucumber, peeled and seeded

¼ cup minced red onion

WELL ahead of time, make the dressing so the flavors can blend. Whisk together the olive oil, vinegar, oregano, salt, and cayenne. Place the mustard and cumin seeds in a dry, heavy-bottomed skillet over medium heat. Shake the pan frequently for 1–2 minutes, until the seeds begin to pop. Stir the hot seeds into the oil mixture (they will sizzle). Add the dried tomato and cilantro. Stir, cover, and set aside at room temperature for up to several hours, until you are ready to assemble the salad.

Roast the bell pepper under a hot broiler, on a grill, or over an open flame on the stovetop. Turn frequently until skin is charred black. Transfer pepper to a plastic or paper bag, close, and set aside for about 15 minutes. When cooled, remove from the bag and peel off the charred skin. Discard the stem, seeds, and white membranes. Dice the pepper and set aside.

Meanwhile, heat 3 cups of water in a covered saucepan until boiling. Stir in the couscous, salt, and garlic. Immediately cover, remove from the heat, and let stand 5 minutes. Transfer couscous to a serving bowl and fluff with a fork. Add the roasted bell pepper to the bowl. Grate the cucumber into the bowl and add the onion. Toss together the vegetables and couscous. Stir the dressing vigorously and add to the salad. Toss to distribute everything evenly.

NOTE: If the dried tomatoes are too dry to mince, soak them in hot water 15–30 minutes. Drain the tomatoes well and mince them.

EACH SERVING PROVIDES:
342 calories, 9g protein, 10g fat, 3g dietary fiber
53g carbohydrate, 257mg sodium, 0mg cholesterol

Bulgur with Tomatoes, Mint, and Toasted Pine Nuts

ALMOST INSTANT

The fresh mint and pine nuts add distinctive flavors in this twist on traditional Middle Eastern tabbouleh salad.

YIELD: 6 SIDE-DISH SERVINGS

The salad
1 cup uncooked bulgur wheat
1½ pounds fresh pear tomatoes (about 9 medium)
¼ cup pine nuts
3 green onions, minced
½ cup minced fresh mint leaves
1 cup minced fresh parsley leaves
6 large butter lettuce leaves

The dressing
3 tablespoons extra-virgin olive oil
3 tablespoons rice wine vinegar
¼ teaspoon salt
Several grinds pepper

BRING 2 cups of water to a boil and stir in the bulgur. Cover, reduce heat to low, and simmer for 15 minutes. Let stand an additional 5 minutes before removing the lid. Turn into a bowl and allow to cool for a few minutes. Meanwhile, core, seed, and chop the tomatoes and set aside in a bowl.

Place the pine nuts in a dry, heavy-bottomed skillet over medium heat. Shake the pan frequently as they toast. Watch carefully and remove the pine nuts from the pan when they begin to brown. Set aside.

Toss together the bulgur, tomatoes, green onions, mint, and parsley. Whisk the dressing ingredients in a small bowl, then pour over the bulgur. Toss well to combine. You may prepare the salad ahead of time and refrigerate, but bring it to room temperature before serving. To serve, mound the salad on lettuce leaves and garnish with the pine nuts.

EACH SERVING PROVIDES:

226 calories, 6g protein, 13g fat, 5g dietary fiber
25g carbohydrate, 112mg sodium, 0mg cholesterol

SUMMERY MIDDLE·EAST SUPPER

Curried Eggplant and Garbanzo Patties, page 254

Bulgur with Tomatoes, Mint, and
Toasted Pine Nuts, page 42

Cauliflower Sautéed with Peaches
and Cardamom, page 98

Raw cucumber sticks

Hot or iced mint tea

Rice and Lentil Salad with Pimiento-Stuffed Olives

This salad is best made early in the day, or even the night before you plan to serve it. The preparation is easy, but some time is required for the flavors to blend. Hearty and filling, this distinctive salad is absolutely delicious as a luncheon main course for 6 or a side dish for about 10 at a picnic or potluck.

YIELD: 6 MAIN-DISH SERVINGS

The salad
1 cup uncooked brown basmati rice
2 cloves garlic, minced
⅛ teaspoon salt
Several grinds black pepper
1 cup dried brown lentils
1 small white onion, halved
2 bay leaves
1 cup sliced pimiento-stuffed green olives

The dressing
3 tablespoons extra-virgin olive oil
2 tablespoons white wine vinegar
1 tablespoon Dijon mustard
1 teaspoon dried thyme, crushed
Several grinds black pepper
2 shallots, minced

Bring 2 cups of water to a boil. Add the rice, garlic, salt, and pepper and return to a boil. Cover, reduce heat to very low, and simmer 25–30 minutes, until the water is absorbed and the rice is tender. Allow the rice to stand in the covered pan for

10 minutes, then transfer it to a bowl and set it in the refrigerator to cool a bit.

Meanwhile, sort through the lentils, discarding any foreign objects you may find, and rinse. Bring 4 cups of water, along with the onion and bay leaves, to a boil, then add the lentils. Return to a boil, reduce the heat to medium-low, cover, and simmer 15–20 minutes, until the lentils are barely tender. They will become mushy if overcooked. Drain the lentils and discard the onion and bay leaves. Set the lentils aside to cool.

Whisk together the oil, vinegar, mustard, thyme, and pepper, then stir in the shallots. In a serving bowl, gently combine the cooled lentils and rice with the dressing and the olives. Refrigerate for several hours or overnight to allow the flavors to blend, but bring the salad to room temperature before serving.

EACH SERVING PROVIDES:

316 calories, 11g protein, 11g fat, 6g dietary fiber
45g carbohydrate, 775mg sodium, 0mg cholesterol

Black-Eyed Peas, Corn, and Toasted Walnuts with Spicy/Sweet Vinaigrette

ALMOST INSTANT

Here is a beautiful and scrumptious combination of beans and vegetables with a Southwestern flair. You may toss everything together and serve the salad immediately, or allow the vegetables to marinate for a few hours before tossing in the walnuts. If you're using fresh corn, you will need to purchase about 3 large ears.

YIELD: 6 SIDE-DISH SERVINGS

The dressing
¼ cup fresh-squeezed orange juice
¼ cup whole grain mustard
2 tablespoons apple cider vinegar
1 tablespoon brown rice syrup
Scant pinch salt
Several grinds black pepper
1 tablespoon olive oil

The salad
⅔ cup coarsely chopped raw walnuts
1½ cups fresh or frozen corn kernels
1½ cups freshly cooked or canned black-eyed peas, drained
⅔ cup minced red cabbage
⅓ cup minced white onion
⅓ cup minced green bell pepper
⅓ cup minced fresh parsley leaves

WHISK together the orange juice, mustard, vinegar, brown rice syrup, salt, and pepper until well combined. Whisk in the oil. Set aside so the flavors can blend while you assemble the salad ingredients.

Place the walnuts in a single layer in a dry, heavy-bottomed skillet over medium-high heat. Shake the pan frequently as the nuts brown and begin to emit a wonderful roasted aroma. When the nuts are golden brown, remove them from the pan and set aside until needed.

If using fresh corn, cut the kernels from the ears of corn to measure 1½ cups. Parboil or steam for 4–5 minutes, until tender. If using frozen corn, thaw under hot water or in the microwave until all ice crystals have melted and the corn is room temperature.

Toss the black-eyed peas, cabbage, onion, bell pepper, and parsley with the corn. Combine with the dressing and walnuts and serve immediately, or allow the beans and vegetables to marinate for up to a few hours at room temperature and toss in the walnuts just before serving.

EACH SERVING PROVIDES:
187 calories, 6g protein, 9g fat, 6g dietary fiber
24g carbohydrate, 101mg sodium, 0mg cholesterol

Sweet Potatoes, Wheat Berries, and Peppers with Tomato Chive Vinaigrette

This salad requires some forethought because the wheat berries must soak for a long while before cooking. Also, make the dressing well ahead of time so its flavor can develop. Consider it a good make-ahead dish for a special occasion. Cook the wheat berries, grill the sweet potatoes and peppers, toast the pumpkin seeds, and whisk up the dressing. Then relax for a few hours, or concentrate on other parts of the meal. Just before dinner time, toss all the ingredients together. Delicious!

YIELD: 8 SIDE-DISH SERVINGS

The salad
⅔ cup wheat berries
2 tablespoons hulled raw pumpkin seeds
1½ pounds fresh mild peppers (such as bell, anaheim, or wax)
1 pound sweet potato (about 1 large)
1½ teaspoons olive oil

The dressing
½ cup tomato juice
2 tablespoons apple cider vinegar
½ teaspoon ground allspice
⅛ teaspoon salt
Pinch cayenne
3 tablespoons minced fresh chives

SOAK the wheat berries for 6 to 8 hours in 3 cups cold water. Drain and rinse, then put in a saucepan with 2 cups fresh water. Bring to a simmer over medium-high heat. Reduce heat to low, cover, and simmer about an hour, until the wheat berries are tenderized and some have popped open. They will still have a chewy texture. Turn off the heat and allow to stand, covered, 10 minutes. Drain and refrigerate for an hour or so before assembling the salad.

Meanwhile, preheat a coal or gas grill to medium. While it is heating, place the pumpkin seeds in a single layer in a dry, heavy-bottomed skillet over medium-high heat. Shake the pan frequently and watch closely. The nuts are ready when most of them have popped and are golden brown. Immediately remove the seeds from the pan and set aside.

Place the whole peppers on the grill and turn every few minutes until their skin is charred almost uniformly black. (Alternatively, you may roast the peppers under a preheated broiler or over an open flame on the stovetop.) Transfer the charred peppers to a plastic or paper bag and fold the bag closed. Set aside to steam for 10 minutes or so—the peppers will finish cooking in the bag.

Scrub the sweet potato and cut crosswise into ¼-inch slices. Rub both sides of the potato slices with the olive oil, then place them on the grill. Cook, turning frequently, for 10–15 minutes, until the slices are tender and well-browned. Remove from the grill and allow to cool for a few minutes before cutting the slices into 3 or 4 strips each. Set aside at room temperature.

When the peppers are cool enough to handle, remove them from the bag and peel off the charred skin. Discard the stems, seeds, and white membranes, and coarsely chop the peppers into 1-inch pieces.

(continued)

(Sweet Potatoes, Wheat Berries, and Peppers with Tomato Chive Vinaigrette, *continued*)

Whisk together the dressing ingredients or shake in a tightly closed jar until well combined. Set aside at room temperature. To assemble the salad, combine the wheat berries, sweet potato strips, peppers, and dressing. Toss to combine and mound the salad onto a serving platter. Chop the toasted pumpkin seeds and distribute over the salad. Garnish with whole chive spears, if desired. Serve at room temperature.

EACH SERVING PROVIDES:

155 calories, 5g protein, 2g fat, 4g dietary fiber

32g carbohydrate, 107mg sodium, 0mg cholesterol

Mushroom, Radish, and Celery Salad with Lemon and Garlic

ALMOST INSTANT

This simple dish offers lovely colors, a pleasing combination of textures, and light and lively flavor—a wonderful spring-time combination! Be sure to use the celery's inner, yellowish stalks (the celery heart), which have a delicate, sweet flavor and aren't stringy.

YIELD: 4 SIDE-DISH SERVINGS

1 tablespoon extra-virgin olive oil
2 tablespoons fresh-squeezed lemon juice
1 clove garlic, minced
¼ teaspoon salt
Several grinds black pepper
¼ cup minced fresh Italian parsley leaves
½ pound thinly sliced button mushrooms (2 cups)
1 cup thinly sliced red radishes
1 cup thinly sliced celery hearts
4 large butter lettuce leaves

WHISK together the oil, lemon juice, garlic, salt, and pepper until well combined. Stir in the parsley and set aside at room temperature. Combine the sliced vegetables in a bowl. Pour on the dressing and toss again. Serve immediately, or allow to stand at room temperature, tossing occasionally, for an hour or two. Serve atop the lettuce leaves.

EACH SERVING PROVIDES:
60 calories, 2g protein, 4g fat, 2g dietary fiber
6g carbohydrate, 171mg sodium, 0mg cholesterol

Potatoes and Artichokes with Mustard Caper Vinaigrette

This delicious salad combines many of the favorite flavors of the Mediterranean. Using freshly cooked artichokes instead of canned adds depth and subtlety of flavor—hallmarks of real Italian cooking. Trimming the artichokes is the most time-consuming preparation task for this dish, but it goes quickly once you get the hang of it. The marinated vegetables can be made several hours in advance and held at room temperature until serving time.

YIELD: 6 SIDE-DISH SERVINGS

2 tablespoons white wine vinegar
2 teaspoons Dijon mustard
2 cloves garlic, minced
3 tablespoons extra-virgin olive oil
2 tablespoons capers, drained and minced
6 tablespoons lemon juice or vinegar
3 pounds artichokes (6 medium)
¾ pound tiny red potatoes
⅓ cup minced red bell pepper
½ cup minced fresh Italian parsley leaves
3 cups bite-sized mixed salad greens
6 fresh lemon wedges

STIR together the vinegar, mustard, and garlic until well blended, then whisk in the olive oil. Stir in the capers. Set aside at room temperature while you prepare the vegetables.

Prepare acidulated water in a large bowl by combining 2 quarts of cold water with the lemon juice or vinegar. Set aside near your work surface.

Trim the artichokes, working with 1 artichoke at a time. Use your hands to snap off all outer leaves until you get down to the pale leaves at the center. (The leaves may be steamed and eaten separately or reserved for another use.) Use a sharp paring knife to cut off the leaf tips, leaving only the base and yellowish green leaves. Cut off ¼ inch of the stem end, then peel the stem and the bottom of each artichoke. Proceed until you have trimmed all the artichokes in this manner, dropping each artichoke into the acidulated water as you finish.

Remove the artichoke "hearts" from the water one at a time and quarter them from stem to top. Use a paring knife or melon baller to scrape out the fuzzy "choke" portion. Finally, slice each quarter lengthwise into thirds or fourths, depending on their size. You want wedges about ¼ inch thick. As you go, drop the artichoke pieces back into the acidulated water.

Scrub the potatoes well; do not peel. Slice them crosswise into ¼-inch-thick pieces. Pour an inch of water into the bottom of two medium-size saucepans. Put the potatoes in one, the artichokes in the other, and cover both pans. Place both pans over medium-high heat and cook the vegetables until fork-tender but not soft, about 6–8 minutes. Test frequently; the texture of the vegetables is important to the success of the dish.

When cooked, drain the artichokes and potatoes, and rinse with cold water. Drain thoroughly and toss together in a serving bowl, along with the bell pepper. Toss again with the dressing and set aside to marinate at room temperature for up to several hours, if you wish.

When ready to serve, toss the vegetable mixture with the parsley and greens. Serve with a wedge of lemon at each plate, and pass the pepper grinder.

EACH SERVING PROVIDES:
192 calories, 6g protein, 8g fat, 9g dietary fiber
29g carbohydrate, 232mg sodium, 0mg cholesterol

Golden Beet, Jicama, and Cucumber Salad with Fresh Mint

This is a wonderfully crunchy salad, and the cucumber and mint both lend a refreshing flavor. Serve it with an Asian-inspired menu, or one that has its origins in the Southwest.

YIELD: 8 SIDE-DISH SERVINGS

4 medium golden beets (about 2¼ pounds)
1 large cucumber, peeled, seeded, and diced
2 cups peeled and diced jicama (about ¾ pound)
1 medium red onion, thinly sliced
¼ cup minced fresh mint
¼ cup seasoned rice wine vinegar
⅛ teaspoon salt

RINSE the beets and place them on a steamer rack in a saucepan that has a tight-fitting lid. Add about 3 inches of water, cover the pan, and cook over medium-high heat about 25 minutes, until each beet is tender all the way through. Rinse the beets under cold water, drain, and set them aside to cool.

Place the cucumber in a medium-size bowl. Add the jicama, onion, and mint, and toss to combine. Peel and dice the beets and toss them with the jicama mixture. Whisk together the vinegar and salt in a small bowl, and pour over the salad. Toss again. Chill, covered, in the refrigerator for several hours to develop the flavors. Serve cold.

EACH SERVING PROVIDES:
100 calories, 3g protein, 0.4g fat, 5.3g dietary fiber
22.4g carbohydrate, 400mg sodium, 0mg cholesterol

SOUPS AND STEWS

SOUPS AND STEWS

Rice, Pea, and Mushroom Soup with Fresh Oregano

Barley Cannellini Bean Stew with Broccoli and Tomatoes

Winter Squash and Cauliflower Soup with Rosemary
and Marsala

Sautéed Ginger Greens and Soba in Miso Broth

Spicy Chili Beans with Tempeh and Dried Peaches

Black Bean Soup with Epazote and Lime

Roasted Corn Soup with Fresh Basil

Hominy and Tomatillo Stew with Pumpkin Seeds

Okra, Corn, and Tofu Gumbo

Curried Spinach with Tomatoes and Pureed Garbanzos

Potato, Zucchini, and Olive Stew with Garlic, Jalapeños,
and Tomatoes

Chilled Asparagus Orange Soup with Pistachios

Green Gazpacho

Homemade Vegetable Stock

T HE FRAGRANT STEAM rising from a simmering stockpot captures everyone in the house and draws them to the kitchen. Soups work a certain magic, and we enjoy them throughout the year.

Grains, beans, vegetables, herbs, and a good stock are the humble building blocks of our favorite vegan soups and stews. The possible combinations are nearly infinite, and the results can be simple or complex, refreshing or hearty, served hot or cold.

Most of the dishes in this chapter can serve as a meal in a bowl, though smaller portions may be served to launch a multi-course feast. With their interesting colors and textures and delightful aromas and flavors, these soups and stews are likely to become cherished comfort foods at your house, as they have at ours.

Rice, Pea, and Mushroom Soup with Fresh Oregano

This soup was inspired by *Risi e Bisi* (Rice and Peas), a beloved Venetian dish. Our version is made from simple, inexpensive ingredients available year-round. Fix it anytime you want a meal that is quick to prepare, hearty, and warming. For an extra special treat, make the soup with field mushrooms (such as chanterelles or porcini) instead of, or in addition to, supermarket button mushrooms.

YIELD: 4 MAIN-DISH SERVINGS

2 tablespoons olive oil
1 medium yellow onion, diced
½ teaspoon dried rosemary, crushed
½ pound button mushrooms, sliced (2 cups)
3 cloves garlic, minced
½ teaspoon salt
Several grinds black pepper
7 cups Homemade Vegetable Stock (see NOTE)
1 cup uncooked long-grain white rice (not "converted")
2 cups frozen shelled peas
2 tablespoons minced fresh oregano leaves

HEAT the olive oil over medium heat in a stockpot. Sauté the onion with the rosemary for 5 minutes, stirring often. The onion will begin to brown. Add the mushrooms, garlic, salt, and pepper, and stir and sauté about 2 minutes, then add the stock. Cover and bring to a boil over high heat, then stir in the rice. Return to a boil, reduce heat to medium and simmer, uncovered, 15 minutes, stirring occasionally. Add the peas and oregano, and continue to cook until rice is tender, about 5 minutes. Serve hot.

NOTE: If you do not have Homemade Vegetable Stock on hand, make some using the directions on page 84, or dissolve 2 large low-sodium vegetable broth cubes in 7 cups of hot water.

EACH SERVING PROVIDES:
366 calories, 9g protein, 8g fat, 4g dietary fiber
64g carbohydrate, 666mg sodium, 0mg cholesterol

Barley Cannellini Bean Stew with Broccoli and Tomatoes

This simple and nutritious bean stew brings us the flavors of southern Italy. It is hearty and warming—a perfect winter soup.

YIELD: 6 MAIN-DISH SERVINGS

2 tablespoons canola oil
3 cloves garlic, minced
1 large yellow onion, chopped
1 can (28 ounces) crushed tomatoes
4 cups Homemade Vegetable Stock (see NOTE)
1 cup dried cannellini beans
¾ cup uncooked barley
2 cups chopped broccoli
2 medium carrots, chopped
3 tablespoons fresh oregano leaves
⅛ teaspoon salt
Several grinds black pepper

HEAT the oil in a stockpot over medium heat and sauté the garlic and onion for several minutes, then add the tomatoes, vegetable stock, and beans. Bring to a boil, reduce the heat to medium, and simmer, stirring occasionally, 25 minutes. Meanwhile, put the barley in a small pan with a tight-fitting lid. Add 2 cups of hot water, cover, and let stand for 20 minutes. Add the barley to the soup, along with its soaking liquid, return to a simmer, and cook an additional 20 minutes over medium heat. Stir in the broccoli, carrots, oregano, salt, and pepper, plus 2 cups of hot water, and cook 20–25 minutes longer until the vegetables and beans are tender. Serve immediately.

NOTE: If you do not have Homemade Vegetable Stock on hand, make some using the directions on page 84, or dissolve 1½ large low-sodium vegetable broth cubes in 4 cups of hot water.

EACH SERVING PROVIDES:

293 calories, 13g protein, 6g fat, 9g dietary fiber
49g carbohydrate, 126mg sodium, 0mg cholesterol

A MEAL IN A BOWL

Some of our favorite casual meals consist solely of a brimming bowl of thick soup or hearty stew. In the tradition of Italian *minestrone*—literally "big soup"— they combine grains, beans, and vegetables in a single pot and are particularly appealing during the cold weather months.

Winter Squash and Cauliflower Soup with Rosemary and Marsala

This tangy/sweet soup hits the spot when autumn's chill and the new crop of winter squashes simultaneously arrive. Once the squash is peeled and diced, most of the work is done. Bread and a bowl of olives round out the meal in an authentic Italian manner. One large acorn squash (about 1½ pounds) will yield about 4 cups of diced flesh, but Hubbard or butternut squash can also be used.

YIELD: 6 MAIN-DISH SERVINGS

1½ pounds winter squash
1 tablespoon olive oil
1 medium yellow onion, diced
¼ teaspoon dried red chili flakes
5 cloves garlic, minced
2 teaspoons dried rosemary, crushed
⅛ teaspoon salt
4 cups Homemade Vegetable Stock (see NOTE)
1 can (28 ounces) whole tomatoes
2 cups diced cauliflower
¾ cup dried small shell pasta
⅓ cup Marsala

CUT the squash in half and scrape out the seeds and stringy pulp. Peel the squash and dice the flesh to measure 4 cups. Heat the olive oil in a stockpot over medium-high heat for a moment, then add the onion and chili flakes. Stir and sauté about 2 minutes, then stir in the squash, garlic, rosemary, and salt. Sauté about 7 minutes, stirring frequently, until the squash and onions are beginning to brown. Add the stock and the tomatoes with their juice. Cover and bring to a boil over high heat. Stir in the cauliflower, pasta, and Marsala, and bring back to a boil over high heat. Reduce heat to medium-high to maintain a strong simmer and cook about 12 minutes, until cauliflower is fork-tender and pasta is al dente. Serve very hot in warmed bowls.

NOTE: If you do not have Homemade Vegetable Stock on hand, make some using the directions on page 84, or dissolve 1½ large low-sodium vegetable broth cubes in 4 cups of hot water.

EACH SERVING PROVIDES:
186 calories, 5g protein, 3g fat, 4g dietary fiber
34g carbohydrate, 388mg sodium, 0mg cholesterol

Sautéed Ginger Greens and Soba in Miso Broth

This is our version of a classic Japanese noodle soup, hearty and warming. It makes a perfect winter lunch—in Japan, it might even be served for breakfast on a chilly morning. If you can't find green tea soba, substitute buckwheat soba or your favorite dried Asian noodle. This dish comes together quickly, despite all the steps, so assemble all your ingredients before you begin.

YIELD: 4 MAIN-DISH SERVINGS

1 medium white onion
½ pound broccoli
½ medium green bell pepper
1 small carrot
½ pound bok choy
¼ cup mirin
1 tablespoon grated fresh ginger
2 tablespoons low-sodium soy sauce
8 ounces dried green tea soba
1½ teaspoons dark sesame oil
1½ teaspoons canola oil
¼ teaspoon dried red chili flakes
3 cups Homemade Vegetable Stock (see NOTE)
3 tablespoons light-colored miso

BRING 4 quarts of water to a boil in a stockpot. Meanwhile, halve the onion lengthwise, then thickly slice each half. Cut the broccoli into thin spears. Sliver the bell pepper and cut the carrot into thin matchsticks. Coarsely chop the bok choy keeping the stem portion separate from the leaves. Set the vegetables aside. Stir together the mirin, ginger, 1 tablespoon of the soy sauce, and ¼ cup water. Set aside.

Stir the soba into the boiling water and return to a rolling boil. Add a cup of cold water and bring back to a boil. Repeat this process 2 more times, then turn off the heat, cover the pot, and allow to stand 10 minutes.

Meanwhile, heat the oils in a wok or skillet over medium heat. Add the onion and chili flakes and cook, stirring frequently, about 3 minutes. Add the broccoli, bell pepper, carrot, and the stem portion of the bok choy. Stir-fry about 3 minutes, add the leaves of the bok choy, and stir-fry about 2 minutes longer. Add the mirin mixture to the wok and stir-fry another 4–5 minutes, until the vegetables are fork-tender and beginning to brown. Turn down the heat if the vegetables seem to be browning too quickly.

While you are cooking the vegetables, gently heat the stock with the remaining 1 tablespoon soy sauce until steaming. Keep hot, but don't allow the stock to simmer. Whisk the miso into ¼ cup water and set aside.

To assemble the dish, drain the soba. Stir the miso into the hot stock and taste it. Add a little more soy sauce or salt, if needed. Divide the stock between 4 deep serving bowls. Put a portion of the cooked soba into each of the bowls and top with the sautéed vegetables and their pan juices. Serve immediately.

NOTE: If you do not have Homemade Vegetable Stock on hand, make some according to the directions on page 84, or dissolve 1 large low-sodium vegetable broth cube in 3 cups of hot water.

EACH SERVING PROVIDES:
311 calories, 11g protein, 5g fat, 8g dietary fiber
52g carbohydrate, 1066mg sodium, 0mg cholesterol

Spicy Chili Beans with Tempeh and Dried Peaches

This hearty stew rivals anyone's favorite chili in both texture and flavor.

YIELD: 8 MAIN-DISH SERVINGS

2 cups dried pinto beans
1 cup dried adzuki beans
3 bay leaves
1 teaspoon dried red chili flakes
6 cloves garlic, coarsely chopped
2 tablespoons olive oil
1 large white onion, coarsely chopped
1 tablespoon dried oregano
1 tablespoon mustard seeds
2 teaspoons ground cumin
2 teaspoons chili powder
8 ounces tempeh, crumbled
½ teaspoon salt
1 can (4 ounces) whole green chiles
½ cup fresh-squeezed orange juice
1 can (28 ounces) whole tomatoes, chopped
⅓ cup chopped dried peaches or apricots
1 tablespoon molasses

SORT the beans carefully and discard any small stones or discolored beans. Soak the two types of beans together in plenty of water at room temperature several hours or overnight. Drain off the soaking water and rinse the beans, then place in a stockpot with 10 cups of water, bay leaves, chili flakes, and half of the chopped garlic. Simmer over low heat until beans are barely tender—about 1 to 1½ hours—adding more hot water, if necessary, to keep the beans submerged.

Meanwhile, heat the olive oil in a large skillet over medium heat. Sauté the onion, the remaining garlic, oregano, mustard seeds, cumin, chili powder, and tempeh. Add ¼ teaspoon of the salt and stir and sauté until the onion is becoming limp and the tempeh is nicely browned, about 10 minutes.

Remove the seeds and membrane from the chiles and slice them crosswise into thin strips. When the beans are tender, remove the bay leaves and stir in the remaining ¼ teaspoon salt. Add the tempeh mixture, orange juice, tomatoes and their juice, green chile strips, peaches, and molasses. Simmer, stirring frequently, for 20 minutes. Serve hot.

EACH SERVING PROVIDES:

382 calories, 22g protein, 7g fat, 8g dietary fiber
62g carbohydrate, 293mg sodium, 0mg cholesterol

Black Bean Soup with Epazote and Lime

This soup gains its unique flavor from epazote, an herb commonly used in traditional dishes from the central and southern regions of Mexico. Epazote is easy to grow in North America and will survive year-round if brought indoors during the winter. Mexican specialty food stores carry it, fresh and dried.

YIELD: 4 MAIN-DISH SERVINGS

1 cup dried black beans
8 cups Homemade Vegetable Stock (see NOTE)
2 tablespoons canola oil
3 cloves garlic, minced
1 medium yellow onion, diced
1 medium red bell pepper, diced
2 ribs celery, chopped
1 teaspoon cumin seeds
1 teaspoon coriander seeds
1 teaspoon dried oregano
1 teaspoon chili powder
2 bay leaves
$\frac{1}{4}$ teaspoon black pepper
2 tablespoons minced fresh epazote leaves
2 tablespoons fresh-squeezed lime juice
$\frac{1}{2}$ teaspoon salt

RINSE and sort the beans, then put them in a large stockpot and cover with boiling water. Cover the pot and allow the beans to soak for 1 hour. Drain into a colander. Return the beans to the stockpot and add the vegetable stock. Bring to a boil over high heat, then reduce the heat to medium-low and simmer, uncovered, for 30 minutes.

Meanwhile, heat the oil in a large skillet over medium heat and sauté the garlic, onion, bell pepper, celery, cumin, coriander, oregano, chili powder, bay leaves, and black pepper for 10 minutes, stirring frequently. Add the sautéed vegetables to the beans and simmer for 30 minutes before adding the epazote, lime juice, and salt. Cook an additional 15 minutes or so, until the beans are tender. Remove bay leaves. Serve immediately.

NOTE: If you do not have Homemade Vegetable Stock on hand, make some according to the directions on page 84, or dissolve 2 large low-sodium vegetable broth cubes in 8 cups of hot water.

EACH SERVING PROVIDES:
275 calories, 10g protein, 8g fat, 6g dietary fiber
41g carbohydrate, 657mg sodium, 0mg cholesterol

SIMPLE TEX·MEX MENU
••

Black Bean Soup with Epazote and Lime, page 68

Spinach, Kiwi, and Grapefruit Salad with Cilantro
Sherry Vinaigrette, page 32

Warmed corn tortillas

Chilled amber ale

Roasted Corn Soup with Fresh Basil

When corn is abundant and you want a new way to enjoy it, try this delicious soup. If you do not have a grill, place the corn under a broiler, about six inches from the heat, and cook as directed in the recipe.

YIELD: 4 MAIN-DISH SERVINGS

1 medium bulb garlic
6 ears corn with husks intact
3 cups Homemade Vegetable Stock (see NOTE)
1 medium russet potato, peeled, and cubed
⅔ cup rice milk
¼ teaspoon salt
Several grinds black pepper
½ cup fresh basil leaves, chiffonade (see NOTE)

PREHEAT a coal or gas grill to medium-high. Lightly oil the unpeeled garlic bulb and place it on the grill. Cook for about 45 minutes, until soft.

Meanwhile, soak the corn, husks and all, in cold water for about 15 minutes. Remove from the water, pat dry, then place on the grill with the garlic. Grill for about 30 minutes, turning occasionally, until the husks are slightly charred. Remove the garlic and corn from the grill and set aside. When cool enough to handle, shuck the corn, discarding the husks and silks. Cut the kernels from the cob, reserving the cobs.

In a stockpot, combine the broth, potato, and reserved corn cobs. Bring to a boil over high, reduce the heat to medium, cover, and simmer for about 20 minutes, until the potatoes are tender. Remove from the heat and discard the corn cobs.

Meanwhile, squeeze the garlic from its papery skin into the bowl of a food processor, discarding the skin. Add the corn kernels. With a slotted spoon, lift the potatoes from the cooking broth and add them to the food processor. Process, adding the cooking broth as needed to create a smooth but quite thick puree. (Pureeing may need to be done in 2 batches.) Return to the pan and stir in the rice milk, basil, salt, and pepper, then gently reheat. Garnish with basil or mint sprigs, if desired.

NOTE: If you do not have Homemade Vegetable Stock on hand, make some according to the directions on page 84, or dissolve 1½ large low-sodium vegetable broth cubes in 3 cups of hot water.

NOTE: To cut fresh herbs chiffonade style, stack several clean and dried leaves, roll tightly from one long side to the other, and slice crosswise as thinly as possible with a sharp knife.

EACH SERVING PROVIDES:
185 calories, 14g protein, 2g fat, 5g dietary fiber
43g carbohydrate, 171mg sodium, 0mg cholesterol

Hominy and Tomatillo Stew with Pumpkin Seeds

Here is our version of a classic Mexican comfort food—green pozole. The flavors are mouth-filling, the texture chunky and satisfying. Hominy, the primary ingredient, is a specially prepared dried corn. Canned hominy is available in well-stocked supermarkets.

YIELD: 4 MAIN-DISH SERVINGS

½ cup hulled raw pumpkin seeds
1 pound fresh tomatillos (about 10–12)
1 cup firmly packed chopped fresh sorrel leaves
3½ cups Homemade Vegetable Stock (see NOTE)
2 medium serrano chiles, chopped
1 clove garlic, chopped
1 tablespoon canola oil
3 cups white hominy (1 can [28 ounces], drained)
¼ teaspoon salt

Topping options
Minced white onion
Diced avocado tossed with lemon juice
Chopped raw or pickled jalapeños
Dried oregano
Lime wedges for squeezing into the soup
Diced fresh tomatoes
Minced fresh cilantro leaves
Shredded lettuce

PLACE the pumpkin seeds in a dry, heavy-bottomed skillet over medium-high heat. Toast the seeds, shaking the pan occasionally, about 5 minutes. Seeds will turn golden brown and pop in the pan. Immediately transfer to a plate or bowl to cool. When cool, grind the seeds with a mortar and pestle or in a food processor to a fine meal consistency. Set aside.

Meanwhile, peel the tomatillos. Place the tomatillos in a small saucepan with 1 cup water, cover the pan, and cook over medium heat 10 minutes. Tomatillos will be very soft. Drain the tomatillos briefly and transfer them to a blender. Add the sorrel, 1 cup of the vegetable stock, the chiles, and garlic and puree thoroughly.

Heat the oil in a heavy, deep-walled pan over medium-high heat. Pour the tomatillo puree into the pan through a wire-mesh strainer, pressing with the back of a wooden spoon or rubber spatula to force the mixture through the mesh. The tomatillo seeds will remain in the strainer; discard them. Cook the puree for 5 minutes, stirring frequently. Add the ground pumpkin seeds, reduce heat to low, and cook 10 minutes, occasionally stirring and scraping the bottom of the pan to prevent sticking.

Add the remaining 2½ cups stock, hominy, and salt to the pan. Increase heat to medium-high and cook 15 minutes, stirring occasionally. Meanwhile, prepare the toppings and place them in bowls or plates to serve alongside the pozole. When the soup is done, ladle into bowls and serve hot. Diners may add whatever combination of toppings they like.

NOTE: If you do not have Homemade Vegetable Stock on hand, make some according to the directions on page 84, or dissolve 1 large low-sodium vegetable broth cube in 3½ cups of hot water.

NOTE: Nutrient values exclude toppings.

EACH SERVING PROVIDES:
253 calories, 10g protein, 12g fat, 3g dietary fiber
29g carbohydrate, 684mg sodium, 0mg cholesterol

Okra, Corn, and Tofu Gumbo

Slightly spicy, thick, and rich, this gumbo is one of the great joys of summer. It gets its heat from the green chiles and cayenne, rather than the traditional Cajun sausage. Another diversion from the norm is the use of a "dry" roux, simple browned flour, rather than the oily preparation preferred by Southern cooks. The resulting dish is therefore less fat-laden than its classic cousin. If you are using fresh corn, you will need to purchase 4 large ears to yield about 2 cups of kernels.

YIELD: 8 MAIN-DISH SERVINGS

¼ cup unbleached flour
3 cups uncooked long-grain white rice (not "converted")
Pinch plus ¾ teaspoon salt
1 pound fresh okra
2 cans (4 ounces each) whole green chiles
2 tablespoons canola oil
2 medium white onions, coarsely chopped
2 medium carrots, coarsely chopped
1 medium red bell pepper, finely diced
1 cup chopped celery
1 pound firm tofu, diced
2 cups fresh or frozen corn kernels
1 teaspoon chili powder
¼ teaspoon cayenne
2 teaspoons filé powder
2 medium fresh tomatoes, coarsely chopped

PLACE the flour in a dry, heavy-bottomed skillet over medium heat and brown for 5 minutes, stirring constantly. You must keep the flour moving to prevent it from burning. If the flour begins to blacken (not brown), turn down the heat a little and begin again with fresh flour. When the flour is uniformly dark tan in color, remove it from the pan and set aside.

Bring 6 cups of water to a boil over high heat. Stir in the rice and the pinch of salt. Cover the pot, reduce the heat to very low, and steam 25–30 minutes, until all the liquid has been absorbed and the rice is tender.

Meanwhile, trim off the stem ends of the okra and slice the pods crosswise into 1-inch pieces. Set aside in a bowl. Remove the stems and seeds of the chiles and slice them into long, thin strips. Heat the oil over medium-high heat in a stockpot. Sauté the onions, carrots, bell pepper, and celery for 10 minutes, stirring frequently, until they begin to brown.

Add the tofu, corn kernels, okra, green chiles, chili powder, $\frac{1}{2}$ teaspoon of the salt, and cayenne to the browned vegetable mixture. Lower the heat to medium. Stir and sauté for 10 minutes, then distribute the browned flour evenly over the vegetables and tofu and stir it in. Add $3\frac{1}{2}$ cups of hot water, the remaining $\frac{1}{4}$ teaspoon salt, the filé powder, and the tomatoes. Increase the heat to bring the mixture to a rapid simmer, then reduce the heat to low, cover, and simmer for 10 minutes. Serve hot over hot rice.

EACH SERVING PROVIDES:
380 calories, 13g protein, 7g fat, 5g dietary fiber
69g carbohydrate, 482mg sodium, 0mg cholesterol

Curried Spinach with Tomatoes and Pureed Garbanzos

In this colorful dish, the spinach is very briefly cooked and retains its fresh, bright flavor. Serve it with a tart, leafy salad for a very hearty and satisfying meal.

YIELD: 6 MAIN-DISH SERVINGS

½ teaspoon salt
4 green onions, minced
Several grinds pepper
1½ cups uncooked brown basmati rice
1 can (28 ounces) whole tomatoes
2 cups freshly cooked or canned garbanzo beans, drained
6 cloves garlic, minced
1 teaspoon cumin seeds, crushed
1 teaspoon ground turmeric
½ teaspoon ground ginger
¼ teaspoon fennel seeds, crushed
¼ teaspoon cayenne
2 pounds spinach (about 2½ bunches)
1 tablespoon fresh-squeezed lemon juice
¼ cup minced fresh cilantro leaves

COMBINE 3 cups of water with ¼ teaspoon of the salt, half of the green onions, and the pepper in a medium saucepan over high heat and bring to a boil. Add the rice, bring back to a boil, reduce heat to low, cover, and cook 20–25 minutes, until water is absorbed and rice is tender. Allow to sit, covered, at least 5 additional minutes, then fluff with a fork before serving.

Meanwhile, combine the tomatoes and their juice with the garbanzo beans, garlic, cumin, turmeric, ginger, fennel, cayenne, and the remaining ¼ teaspoon of salt in a large skillet or saucepan over medium-high heat. When it comes to a simmer, reduce heat to medium-low and cook, stirring frequently, 10 minutes. Transfer half the mixture in small batches to a food processor or blender and puree briefly to a chunky sauce consistency. Stir the puree back into the pan.

Meanwhile, carefully wash the spinach, discarding the stems. Place the wet spinach in a large stockpot over medium-high heat, cover, and steam 5 minutes. Transfer it to a colander and rinse with cold water. When the spinach is cool enough to handle, squeeze it gently to remove most of the juice (this can be saved for another use, if you wish, such as soup stock). Chop the spinach coarsely. Stir the spinach, lemon juice, and cilantro into the bean mixture and cook over low heat for 2 minutes, to just heat through. Place portions of rice on warmed serving plates and top with the spinach mixture and the remaining green onions.

EACH SERVING PROVIDES:

323 calories, 13g protein, 4g fat, 8g dietary fiber
63g carbohydrate, 296mg sodium, 0mg cholesterol

FRESHLY COOKED BEANS

Freshly cooked dried beans provide better flavor and texture than canned varieties. If you cover dried beans with boiling water, they need only soak for 2 hours before cooking. After soaking, drain the beans, cover them with fresh water, and boil until tender, but not mushy. Cooking time will vary depending on the type of bean and on its age. One cup of dried beans will yield 2–2½ cups cooked beans. The cooked beans may be cooled, then frozen for up to several months. When necessary, you may use canned beans.

Potato, Zucchini, and Olive Stew with Garlic, Jalapeños, and Tomatoes

This classic Mexican flavor combination—complex, rich, and absolutely delicious—is developed by cooking for quite a long while. The technique, however, is quite simple. The recipe calls for fresh tomatoes. If they are not in season, you may substitute one 28-ounce can of whole tomatoes, drained, and omit the roasting step. Select the smallest potatoes you can find—any variety, or a combination of varieties, will work. Serve the stew with plain steamed rice or Mexican-flavored rice, warm corn tortillas, and a tart green salad. Any leftovers will improve over the course of a couple of days; refrigerate in a tightly covered container and reheat gently but thoroughly.

YIELD: 6 MAIN-DISH SERVINGS

4 pounds fresh tomatoes (about 8 medium)
3 tablespoons olive oil
10 cloves garlic, peeled and left whole
½ medium white onion
1½ cups Homemade Vegetable Stock (see NOTE)
1 cup chopped fresh parsley leaves
⅛ teaspoon salt
1¼ pounds tiny red potatoes
1 pound zucchini (about 3 medium)
1 cup whole pimiento-stuffed green olives, drained
2 teaspoons chopped pickled jalapeños

ROAST the whole tomatoes under a preheated broiler, turning frequently, until their skins are well charred. Remove from the heat and set aside to cool for a few minutes. When the tomatoes are cool enough to handle, cut out the stem ends, peel away and discard most of the blackened skin, and place the tomatoes in a blender.

Meanwhile, heat the oil over medium heat in a heavy-bottomed stockpot or deep Dutch oven. Add the garlic cloves and cook, stirring constantly, until they begin to turn golden brown. This will take only a minute or two. Watch carefully—if the garlic gets too dark, it will taste bitter. Turn off the heat. Remove the garlic cloves from the oil with a slotted spoon and add them to the tomatoes in the blender, along with the onion, stock, parsley, and salt. Puree until smooth.

Strain the puree through a fine-mesh strainer into the pan in which the garlic was cooked; press and stir with a wooden spoon to remove as much of the liquid as possible. Bring to a simmer over medium-high heat, reduce heat to very low, and simmer, stirring frequently, for 20 minutes. The sauce will reduce and thicken considerably.

Meanwhile, scrub the potatoes but do not peel them. Cook the whole potatoes in plenty of rapidly boiling water until they are barely fork-tender, about 10–15 minutes, depending on their size. Drain and set aside. Discard the stems and root ends of the zucchini and slice crosswise into ½-inch rounds.

(continued)

(Potato, Zucchini, and Olive Stew with Garlic, Jalapeños, and Tomatoes, *continued*)

When the sauce has thickened, cut the potatoes in half and stir them into the sauce, along with the zucchini, olives, and jalapeños. Simmer over low heat, stirring frequently, 20 minutes. Serve very hot.

NOTE: If you do not have Homemade Vegetable Stock on hand, make some according to the directions on page 84, or dissolve ½ large low-sodium vegetable broth cube in 1½ cups of hot water.

EACH SERVING PROVIDES:
248 calories, 5g protein, 10g fat, 9g dietary fiber
38g carbohydrate, 683mg sodium, 0mg cholesterol

Chilled Asparagus Orange Soup with Pistachios

Cool soup makes a refreshing light supper or first course at a summer dinner party. This one is particularly delicious.

YIELD: 6 FIRST-COURSE SERVINGS

2 pounds fresh asparagus
2 tablespoons canola oil
2 medium yellow onions, coarsely chopped
1 tablespoon dried tarragon
⅛ teaspoon salt
Pinch cayenne
1 cup fresh-squeezed orange juice
2 tablespoons Madeira
⅓ cup minced unsalted pistachios

REMOVE the tough stem ends of the asparagus and cut into 2-inch pieces. Heat the oil in a stockpot over medium-high heat. Sauté the asparagus, onion, and tarragon for about 5 minutes. Add 2 cups of water, salt, and cayenne and bring to a simmer over high heat. Reduce heat to medium, cover, and cook 15 minutes, until asparagus and onion are very soft. Puree in a blender or food processor until smooth, then stir in the orange juice and Madeira. Chill until a half hour before serving time, then bring it to room temperature. Serve in pretty bowls with minced pistachios sprinkled on top. A thin orange peel curl on each bowl would be the crowning touch.

EACH SERVING PROVIDES:
147 calories, 4g protein, 9g fat, 2g dietary fiber
14g carbohydrate, 57mg sodium, 0mg cholesterol

Green Gazpacho

Bright and lively in both color and flavor, this unconventional variation on a traditional Spanish soup can launch any summer feast.

YIELD: 4 FIRST-COURSE SERVINGS

1 pound fresh tomatillos
1 large cucumber
1 medium green bell pepper
1 medium serrano chile
3 green onions, chopped
¼ cup plus 2 tablespoons minced fresh mint leaves
1 cup fresh bread cubes, crust removed
2 tablespoons extra-virgin olive oil
1 tablespoon red wine vinegar
1 clove garlic, chopped
½ teaspoon salt
½ teaspoon natural granulated sugar
¼ cup finely diced red bell pepper
¼ cup finely diced red radishes
4 lime wedges

BRING 2 cups of water to a boil in a saucepan while you peel off and discard the papery husks of the tomatillos. Place the whole tomatillos in the boiling water, cover, reduce heat to medium, and cook about 8 minutes, until they are quite soft but not falling apart. Drain well and transfer them to a blender. Puree, then strain the puree through a fine mesh strainer into the bowl of a food processor. Press the tomatillos through the strainer with a rubber spatula or wooden spoon to force as much pulp and juice as possible through the mesh.

Peel the cucumber and cut it in half lengthwise. Use a spoon to scrape out the seeds; discard them. Coarsely chop the cucumber and add it to the food processor. Cut the bell pepper in half and discard the seeds, stem, and white membrane. Coarsely chop the bell pepper and add it to the food processor. Discard the stem of the chile and scrape out the seeds for a milder dish. Chop it into a few pieces and add to the food processor. Add the green onions, the ¼ cup mint, the bread, oil, vinegar, garlic, salt, and sugar. Pour in ¾ cup of cold water and puree the mixture thoroughly to achieve a thick, uniform texture. Taste the mixture. If it is too tart, add a bit more sugar. Refrigerate the mixture.

In a small bowl, combine the red bell pepper, radishes, and the remaining 2 tablespoons mint. When ready to serve the soup, thin it if necessary to achieve a thick but not viscous texture by stirring in cold water or vegetable stock a tablespoonful at a time. Ladle the soup into chilled shallow bowls and top with a portion of the bell pepper, radish, and mint mixture. Serve immediately with lime wedges on the side.

EACH SERVING PROVIDES:
143 calories, 3g protein, 8g fat, 4g dietary fiber
17g carbohydrate, 323mg sodium, 0mg cholesterol

Homemade Vegetable Stock

Any vegetable trimmings can be included in the stockpot. This recipe emphasizes seasonings and vegetables commonly used in Italian cooking, but virtually any combination of vegetables, including fresh or dried mushrooms and herbs, will make a good stock. Don't feel compelled to measure precisely; just use about twice as much water as mixed vegetables, by volume, and don't allow a single vegetable to predominate.

YIELD: ABOUT 10 CUPS

2 medium unpeeled russet potatoes, coarsely chopped
2 medium yellow onions, diced
1 medium green bell pepper, diced
1 rib celery, chopped
½ pound mushrooms
2 cups assorted vegetables, chopped (see NOTE)
6 cloves garlic, chopped
2 bay leaves
2 teaspoons dried rosemary
2 teaspoons dried basil
½ teaspoon dried thyme
½ teaspoon peppercorns
¾ teaspoon salt

Put 14 cups of water in a large stockpot over medium-high heat. Add all the vegetables, herbs, peppercorns, and salt, and bring to a boil. Reduce heat to low and simmer, uncovered, 45 minutes. Turn off the heat and allow the mixture to steep for an additional 15–30 minutes before straining into a separate pot or large bowl. Any stock you do not use immediately may be stored for several days in the refrigerator or for several months in the freezer.

NOTE: Good choices for the assorted vegetables would be summer squash, broccoli stalks, spinach or chard stems, and carrots. If you include broccoli or other members of the cabbage family, keep the total quantity of these at no more than 1 cup, as the flavors and aromas of such strong vegetables can dominate the stock.

EACH CUP PROVIDES:

23 calories, 0g protein, 0g fat, 0g dietary fiber
5g carbohydrate, 182mg sodium, 0mg cholesterol

FREEZING STOCK

You don't need to wait until you're cooking soup to make stock. If you have a good supply of fresh vegetables on hand—including trimmings from carrots, potatoes, onions, and the like—make up a batch and freeze it for future use. Freeze measured amounts in labeled glass jars or plastic containers, leaving an inch of head room so the stock can expand. You may also wish to freeze some in ice cube trays for those occasions when only a small amount is called for in a recipe.

SIDE-DISH
VEGETABLES

SIDE-DISH VEGETABLES

Parsley Red Potatoes

Garlic Mashed Potatoes

Spinach with Radicchio and Warm Dried
Tomato Vinaigrette

Artichokes Braised with Garlic and Lemon

Braised Turnips with Chives and Parsley

Cauliflower Sautéed with Peaches and Cardamom

Sherry-Sautéed Broccoli with Fresh Thyme

Sesame Sweet Potato Sauté with Hijiki

Acorn Squash with Tomatoes, Chard, and Pine Nuts

Stovetop Stuffed Tomatoes with Crispy Bread Crumbs

Provençal Skewered Vegetables with Balsamic Marinade

Summer Squash en Papillote with Tex-Mex Seasonings

Steamed Corn with Pimiento and Horseradish

I N TEMPERATE CLIMATES, strolling through a well-tended vegetable garden any time of year can set the culinary imagination soaring. Jewel colors and fanciful shapes please the eye, and crisp, juicy textures tempt the taste buds. Asparagus in springtime, summer eggplants, artichokes in fall, broccoli in winter—every season yields eagerly awaited treasures.

Fresh and succulent vegetables are delicious all by themselves, but creatively enhancing their natural goodness can yield a stunning dish. Even the humblest vegetables are extraordinarily versatile, lending themselves to many different types of preparation and combining well with a world of seasonings.

From rugged potatoes and turnips to the most delicate pod peas—in our kitchens, every vegetable is considered special. We encourage you to think "fresh" when it comes to vegetables and to enjoy these healthful gifts of nature often.

Parsley Red Potatoes

ALMOST INSTANT

This classy and classic all-purpose side dish never fails to satisfy. This type of preparation is also suitable for Yellow Finns or new white potatoes.

YIELD: 4 SIDE-DISH SERVINGS

1 pound red potatoes
1 tablespoon olive oil
¼ cup minced fresh parsley leaves
⅛ teaspoon granulated garlic
A few grinds black pepper
Pinch salt

SCRUB the potatoes and dice them. Drop them into rapidly boiling water and cook about 10 minutes, until tender but not mushy. Drain well and toss in a bowl with the olive oil, then with the parsley, garlic, pepper, and salt. Serve hot.

EACH SERVING PROVIDES:
123 calories, 2g protein, 4g fat, 5g dietary fiber
21g carbohydrate, 43mg sodium, 0mg cholesterol

Garlic Mashed Potatoes

ALMOST INSTANT

The only thing better than standard mashed potatoes is this garlic-laced version. It is positively addicting! You may peel the potatoes if you prefer a perfectly smooth texture, but we usually leave the skins on for the nutrients they hold.

YIELD: 6 SIDE-DISH SERVINGS

2½ pounds russet potatoes (about 5 medium)
6 cloves garlic, peeled and left whole
1 tablespoon olive oil
¼ teaspoon salt
⅛ teaspoon cayenne

SCRUB and dice the potatoes and put them in a large pot with the garlic cloves and enough water to submerge them. Boil until very tender, about 15 minutes after a hard boil has been achieved. Drain, reserving ¼ cup of the cooking water.

Thoroughly mash the potatoes or puree in a food processor with a tablespoon of the reserved potato water, oil, salt, and cayenne. Continue adding potato water a little at a time until the desired consistency is achieved. Serve very hot.

EACH SERVING PROVIDES:
147 calories, 3g protein, 3g fat, 3g dietary fiber
28g carbohydrate, 102mg sodium, 0mg cholesterol

Spinach with Radicchio and Warm Dried Tomato Vinaigrette

ALMOST INSTANT

The radicchio makes a beautiful pink bed for the spinach in this unusual Mediterranean-inspired side dish. Once you have washed the spinach, it comes together in just a few moments.

YIELD: 4 SIDE-DISH SERVINGS

¼ cup minced dried tomato (see NOTE)
2 pounds fresh spinach (about 2½ bunches)
3 tablespoons dry white wine
2 tablespoons balsamic vinegar
1 tablespoon olive oil
1 clove garlic, minced
Pinch salt
A few grinds black pepper
1 teaspoon arrowroot powder or cornstarch
1 cup finely shredded radicchio

CAREFULLY wash the spinach, discarding the stems. Place the wet leaves in a stockpot and cover tightly. Turn the heat on to medium-high and cook the spinach until wilted, about 5 minutes. Transfer to a colander to drain.

Meanwhile, in a very small saucepan, combine the wine, vinegar, olive oil, garlic, salt, and pepper. Bring to a simmer and remove from the heat. Immediately whisk in the arrowroot powder until thickened, then stir in the dried tomato and set aside in a warm spot on the stove.

Make a ring of the radicchio on a serving plate. Mound the spinach in the center and drizzle everything with the warm vinaigrette. Serve hot or at room temperature.

NOTE: Reconstitute the dried tomatoes if they are too dry to mince by soaking them in hot water for 15–30 minutes. Drain the tomatoes well and mince them.

EACH SERVING PROVIDES:
96 calories, 6g protein, 4g fat, 5g dietary fiber
11g carbohydrate, 171mg sodium, 0mg cholesterol

Artichokes Braised with Garlic and Lemon

This recipe works best with medium-size artichokes. The preparation might seem wasteful, as the outer leaves of the artichokes are removed before cooking and only the tender inner leaves and bottoms are used. However, the outer leaves need not be discarded; you can steam them separately and eat them with tofu mayonnaise.

YIELD: 8 SIDE-DISH SERVINGS

6 tablespoons lemon juice or vinegar
4 medium artichokes (about 2 pounds)
¼ cup extra-virgin olive oil
⅓ cup fresh-squeezed lemon juice
5 cloves garlic, minced
¼ teaspoon dried red chili flakes
¼ teaspoon salt
Several grinds black pepper
½ cup minced fresh Italian parsley leaves

PREPARE acidulated water in a large bowl by combining 2 quarts of cold water with the lemon juice or vinegar. Set aside near your work surface.

Trim the artichokes, working with 1 artichoke at a time. Use your hands to snap off all the tough outer leaves until you get down to the pale leaves at the center. Use a sharp knife to cut off the leaf tips, leaving only the base and the bottoms of the yellowish green leaves. Cut off ¼ inch of the stem end, then peel the stem and the bottom of each artichoke. Proceed until you have trimmed all the artichokes in this manner, dropping each artichoke into the acidulated water as you finish. Next, remove the artichoke "hearts" from the water one at a time and quarter them from stem to top. Use a paring knife or melon baller to scrape out the fuzzy "choke" portion. Finally, slice each piece lengthwise into thirds or fourths, depending on their size. You want wedges about ¼ inch thick. As you go, drop the artichoke pieces back into the acidulated water.

Heat the olive oil over medium heat in a large skillet that has a tight-fitting lid. Add ½ cup of fresh water, the lemon juice, garlic, chili flakes, salt, and pepper. Remove the artichoke pieces from the acidulated water and drain them briefly on a kitchen towel. Add them to the pan, toss to coat, cover, and cook 15–20 minutes, until barely fork-tender, stirring at the halfway point. Check frequently toward the end of the cooking time as the liquid will almost be cooked away. If the liquid evaporates before the artichokes are done, add 1–2 tablespoons of water and continue to cook. Remove from the heat, add the parsley, toss, and transfer to a serving dish. Serve hot or at room temperature.

EACH SERVING PROVIDES:

96 calories, 2g protein, 7g fat, 3g dietary fiber
8g carbohydrate, 125mg sodium, 0mg cholesterol

Braised Turnips with Chives and Parsley

ALMOST INSTANT

Unfortunately, turnips seem to have a bad reputation. In reality, they are nourishing—and delicious when properly cooked. Select the smallest turnips you can find, as they are less stringy than the larger ones. Rutabaga or kohlrabi can also be cooked as described in this recipe, and other herbs can be substituted for the parsley and chives, if you prefer.

YIELD: 4 SIDE-DISH SERVINGS

1 pound turnips
1½ tablespoons olive oil
¼ teaspoon salt
Several grinds black pepper
⅓ cup vegetable stock or dry white wine
3 tablespoons minced fresh chives
3 tablespoons minced fresh Italian parsley leaves

PEEL the turnips and chop them into roughly ½-inch cubes. Heat the oil in a skillet over medium-high heat and add the turnips. Sauté about 10 minutes, stirring frequently, until they are browning nicely. Stir in the salt and pepper, then add the stock and immediately cover the pan tightly. Reduce heat to medium-low and cook 10 minutes.

Remove the lid and continue to stir and sauté until all the liquid has evaporated and the turnips are tender, about 3–5 minutes. Stir in the chives and parsley, and transfer to a serving dish. Serve hot or warm.

EACH SERVING PROVIDES:

79 calories, 1g protein, 5g fat, 2g dietary fiber

7g carbohydrate, 226mg sodium, 0mg cholesterol

HEARTY SICILIAN SUPPER

Bucatini with Green Beans, Tomatoes, and Olives, page 124

Braised Turnips with Chives and Parsley, page 96

Mushroom, Radish, and Celery Salad with Lemon and Garlic, page 51

Crusty country bread

Italian Chianti or California Pinot Noir

Cauliflower Sautéed with Peaches and Cardamom

ALMOST INSTANT

The subtle interplay of flavors in this unusual dish is stupendous. It is best enjoyed in the summertime, when fresh peaches are at their peak of sweetness. Canned peaches packed in juice instead of sweet syrup make an acceptable substitute for fresh, but don't bother with mushy winter fruit.

YIELD: 4 SIDE-DISH SERVINGS

4 cups chopped cauliflower
2 medium shallots, slivered
¼ teaspoon salt
¾ pound peaches (2 medium)
   or 1 can (14 ounces) peach slices in natural juice
½ teaspoon ground cardamom
Several grinds black pepper
2 tablespoons minced fresh parsley leaves

COMBINE the cauliflower, shallots, and salt with ⅓ cup water in a heavy-bottomed skillet. Cover and cook over medium heat 7–10 minutes, until the cauliflower is barely fork-tender.

Meanwhile, peel the peaches and slice the flesh from the pits into bite-size chunks. (Alternatively, drain the peach slices and cut them into chunks.)

When the cauliflower is barely tender, stir in the peaches and sprinkle the cardamom and pepper evenly over the contents of the skillet. Cook, stirring gently but frequently, for 3 minutes or so, until the peaches are heated through. Toss with the parsley in a bowl and serve hot or at room temperature.

EACH SERVING PROVIDES:

56 calories, 3g protein, 0g fat, 4g dietary fiber
13g carbohydrate, 151mg sodium, 0mg cholesterol

FRUIT INNOVATIONS

Fruits are not just for snacks and desserts. We occasionally use their natural sweetness and bright colors to enliven savory dishes. The resulting combinations are unexpected and refreshing. Tropical fruits such as mango and papaya, dried fruits like apricots and prunes, summer berries, apples, pears, and peaches lend themselves particularly well to these crossover uses.

Sherry-Sautéed Broccoli with Fresh Thyme

ALMOST INSTANT

This is a lovely broccoli side dish. Set your ingredients out and prepare it just before the rest of the meal is done; overcooked broccoli becomes bitter.

YIELD: 6 SIDE-DISH SERVINGS

2 tablespoons pine nuts
1½ pounds broccoli
2 tablespoons dry sherry
1 tablespoon olive oil
1 clove garlic, minced
1 tablespoon minced fresh thyme leaves
⅛ teaspoon salt
Several grinds black pepper

PLACE the pine nuts in a single layer in a dry, heavy-bottomed skillet over medium-high heat. Cook for several minutes, stirring or shaking the pan frequently, until the nuts begin to brown and emit a roasted aroma. Immediately remove from the pan and set aside.

Cut off and discard the tough stem ends of the broccoli and peel the remaining stalks if they are particularly thick-skinned. Slice the stalks about ¼ inch thick. Chop the florets into uniform, bite-size pieces. Combine the sherry in a small bowl with ¼ cup of water and set aside.

Heat the olive oil over medium heat in a skillet that has a tight-fitting lid and sauté the garlic and broccoli stalks for 2–3 minutes, stirring frequently, until they begin to brown a bit. Stir in the florets, thyme, salt, and pepper. Holding the lid of the pan in one hand, pour in the sherry mixture and immediately cover the pan tightly. Cook for 6–10 minutes. Remove the lid after 4–5 minutes to make sure there is still a little liquid in the pan; you want the broccoli to brown slightly, but not to scorch. If the liquid is gone but the broccoli is not yet tender, add 1–2 tablespoons of water and replace the lid. If the broccoli is tender and there is still liquid in the pan, stir and cook, uncovered, for 1–2 minutes longer, until the liquid has evaporated. Place the broccoli in a warmed serving bowl and top with toasted pine nuts. Serve immediately.

EACH SERVING PROVIDES:

75 calories, 4g protein, 4g fat, 2g dietary fiber
6g carbohydrate, 66mg sodium, 0mg cholesterol

Sesame Sweet Potato Sauté with Hijiki

What a marvelous way to enjoy sweet potatoes! Don't let the exotic combination deter you—it is rich and absolutely delicious, particularly with a teriyaki dish or another Japanese entrée. Hijiki is a dried seaweed available at Asian markets and some natural food stores.

YIELD: 4 SIDE-DISH SERVINGS

⅓ cup dried hijiki seaweed (about ⅓ ounce)
1 teaspoon raw sesame seeds
1¼ pounds red-skinned sweet potatoes (about 2 large)
2 teaspoons canola oil
2 teaspoons dark sesame oil
Pinch salt
Pinch cayenne
2 tablespoons low-sodium soy sauce
2 tablespoons mirin
2 green onions, minced

RINSE the hijiki briefly under cold running water, then place it in 2 cups of warm water and soak for 30 minutes. Lift the hijiki from the water, rinse it again, and drain well.

Meanwhile, toast the sesame seeds in a dry, heavy-bottomed skillet over medium heat, stirring or shaking the pan frequently, until they are lightly browned and emit a wonderful roasted aroma. Immediately remove them from the pan and set aside.

Peel the sweet potatoes, cut them crosswise into ¼-inch slices, then cut the slices into ¼-inch strips. Heat the oils together over medium heat in a heavy-bottomed skillet or wok with a tight-fitting lid. When the oil is hot enough to sizzle a piece of sweet potato, add the sweet potato strips to the pan, along with the salt and cayenne, and stir. Sauté, stirring frequently, for 5 minutes. Add the hijiki and continue to sauté, stirring frequently, 3 minutes.

Meanwhile, combine the soy sauce and mirin with ¼ cup water in a small bowl. Holding the lid of the skillet in one hand, add the soy sauce mixture to the sweet potatoes and immediately cover the pan. Reduce the heat to low and cook for 4 minutes. Remove the lid, increase the heat to medium-high, and cook, stirring constantly, until almost all the liquid is gone and the sweet potatoes are fork-tender—about 2–3 minutes. Transfer to a warmed bowl and serve hot, sprinkled evenly with the green onions and toasted sesame seeds.

EACH SERVING PROVIDES:

225 calories, 3g protein, 6g fat, 5g dietary fiber
40g carbohydrate, 346mg sodium, 0mg cholesterol

Acorn Squash with Tomatoes, Chard, and Pine Nuts

Mediterranean seasonings with winter squash is an unusual combination in this country, but we guarantee you will enjoy this succulent dish. As a bonus, it is packed with health-enhancing nutrients. Its beta-carotene level alone is enough to recommend eating it often.

YIELD: 6 SIDE-DISH SERVINGS

2 tablespoons pine nuts
1¼ pounds acorn squash (1 medium)
1 large red onion
1 pound Swiss chard (about 1½ bunches)
1 tablespoon olive oil
3 cloves garlic, minced
2 teaspoons dried oregano
¼ teaspoon dried red chili flakes
½ teaspoon salt
1¼ cups Homemade Vegetable Stock (see NOTE)
½ pound fresh pear tomatoes (3 medium), diced
2 tablespoons balsamic vinegar

TOAST the pine nuts in a dry, heavy-bottomed skillet over medium-high heat. Stir or shake the pan frequently to prevent scorching. Nuts are done when they are lightly browned and emit a roasted aroma. Immediately remove from the pan, mince them, and set aside.

Cut the acorn squash in half and scoop out and discard the seeds. Slice off and discard the tough rind portion, and coarsely chop the squash. Coarsely chop the red onion. Carefully wash the chard and slice the stem portion. Do not dry the chard leaves; tear them into large pieces and set aside in a colander.

Heat the olive oil in a large, heavy-bottomed skillet with a tight-fitting lid over medium heat and sauté the garlic, oregano, and chili flakes for 1 minute. Add the squash, onion, chard stems, and salt, and sauté, stirring frequently, 5 minutes. Add the vegetable stock, cover, and cook 7 minutes. Remove the lid and stir in the tomatoes. Continue to cook uncovered, stirring frequently, 5–10 minutes, until squash is fork-tender.

Meanwhile, place the wet chard leaves in a saucepan over medium-low heat, cover, and cook 5 minutes, until they wilt. Make a bed of the chard on a warmed platter. Add the vinegar to the squash mixture and gently stir. Spoon the squash evenly over the chard and sprinkle with the pine nuts. Serve hot.

NOTE: If you do not have Homemade Vegetable Stock on hand, make some according to the directions on page 84, or dissolve ½ of a large low-sodium vegetable broth cube in 1¼ cups of hot water.

EACH SERVING PROVIDES:
120 calories, 4g protein, 5g fat, 4g dietary fiber
19g carbohydrate, 378mg sodium, 0mg cholesterol

Stovetop Stuffed Tomatoes with Crispy Bread Crumbs

ALMOST INSTANT

Simple, delicious, and satisfying—these tomatoes are a perfect summer accompaniment to any Mediterranean-inspired main course. Of course, this dish will be only as good as the tomatoes you use, so wait until succulent, vine-ripened tomatoes are available in the garden or at the farmers' markets.

YIELD: 6 SIDE-DISH SERVINGS

1 cup coarse dry bread crumbs
¼ cup minced fresh parsley leaves
1½ teaspoons dried oregano
1½ teaspoons dried basil
2 cloves garlic, minced
¼ teaspoon salt
Several grinds black pepper
3 large, fresh, round tomatoes
¼ cup olive oil

IN a bowl, combine the bread crumbs, parsley, oregano, basil, garlic, salt, and pepper. Cut the tomatoes in half crosswise and squeeze gently over the sink to remove the juicy seed pockets. Holding a tomato half in one hand, use the other hand to gently stuff one-sixth of the crumb mixture into the tomato. A nice thick layer of crumbs should coat the surface of each tomato half.

Heat the oil over medium heat in a skillet large enough to hold all the tomatoes. When the oil is hot enough to sizzle a drop of water, quickly place the tomatoes, stuffed side down, into the oil. Cover the pan loosely and cook for about 3–5 minutes, until the crumbs are crisp and well browned and the tomatoes have softened somewhat. Watch carefully and reduce the heat if the tomatoes seem to be browning too rapidly. Serve hot or at room temperature.

EACH SERVING PROVIDES:

164 calories, 3g protein, 10g fat, 1g dietary fiber
16g carbohydrate, 221mg sodium, 0mg cholesterol

THE PERFECTLY RIPE TOMATO

A vine-ripened tomato at its peak of sweetness is an unsurpassed flavor sensation. If you have only a few square feet of garden space or room for one large pot on a sunny deck, by all means plant tomatoes. Otherwise, seek out a farmers' market for the best quality produce. Supermarket tomatoes are a fair substitute when garden or farm-fresh ones aren't available, but typically they're not fully ripe when purchased. Allow them to ripen in a bowl or basket at room temperature, but out of direct sunlight, for several days before you use them.

Provençal Skewered Vegetables with Balsamic Marinade

At the height of summer, we tend to do a lot of cooking and eating outdoors. This dish brings the Mediterranean into our backyard. To turn this recipe into a delicious main dish for 6, simply include steamed rice, hot bread, and a green leaf salad with garbanzo beans.

YIELD: 12 SIDE-DISH SERVINGS

The marinade
¼ cup olive oil
½ cup balsamic vinegar
3 cloves garlic, minced
2 teaspoons sweet paprika
½ teaspoon dried oregano
⅛ teaspoon salt
Several grinds black pepper

The skewers
24 whole baby red potatoes
2 bulbs garlic
3 medium red bell peppers
2 pounds zucchini (about 6 medium)

COVER 12 wooden skewers with water and soak for 30 minutes. Preheat a coal or gas grill to medium-high. Prepare the marinade by combining all the ingredients and set aside in a high-walled skillet or Dutch oven. Wash the potatoes but leave them whole. (If you can't find the baby red potatoes, cut larger ones into halves or quarters.) Separate the garlic bulbs into individual cloves but do not peel. Add the potatoes and garlic to the marinade and bring to a simmer. Simmer, covered, over medium heat for about 10 minutes. Remove the pan from the heat and set aside to cool. Slip the skins off the garlic.

Meanwhile, cut the peppers into 1½-inch pieces and slice the zucchini crosswise into ¾-inch rounds. On each skewer, place 2 potatoes, 3 slices of zucchini, 3 cloves of garlic, and 3 sections of pepper. Alternate the vegetables as you see fit. Brush the remaining marinade over the skewered vegetables. Grill over medium-high heat for 12 minutes, turning once midway through.

EACH SERVING PROVIDES:

155 calories, 4g protein, 5g fat, 5g dietary fiber
26g carbohydrate, 36mg sodium, 0mg cholesterol

Summer Squash en Papillote with Tex-Mex Seasonings

You may use any type of summer squash for this dish, but it's an especially nice way to prepare patty pans. If you can locate squashes no bigger than a bite or two in size, cook them whole for a stunning feast of sweetness.

YIELD: 4 SIDE-DISH SERVINGS

1 teaspoon cumin seeds
1 teaspoon chili powder
½ teaspoon granulated garlic
⅛ teaspoon salt
Several grinds black pepper
1 pound summer squash
½ medium red bell pepper, slivered
1 small red onion, diced
2 tablespoons minced fresh cilantro leaves
2 tablespoons hulled raw pumpkin seeds

4 pieces (12 × 18 inches each) parchment paper

PREHEAT the oven to 400 degrees F. Use a mortar and pestle or spice grinder to crush the cumin seeds. In a small bowl, stir together the chili powder, cumin seeds, garlic, salt, and pepper. Set aside. Trim the stems off the squashes and cut into bite-size pieces (if using baby squashes, leave them whole).

Fold each piece of parchment in half and crease to create 9 × 12-inch rectangles. Use scissors to cut each folded rectangle into a half-heart shape. Open out the hearts and distribute the squash pieces evenly among the 4 papers, positioning them near the center of each crease. Sprinkle equal portions of the spice mixture evenly over the squash. Lay a quarter of the bell pepper and onion pieces over each portion and sprinkle equal portions of cilantro over each. Close the heart so that the edges of the paper meet. Beginning at the round end, fold over about ½ inch of the paper and crease sharply. Work your way around the shape of the heart, folding in the edges and creasing sharply in overlapping pleats. Twist the pointy end to seal everything tightly in the paper packet. Repeat this process with the remaining packets. Place the packets in a single layer on a baking sheet and bake for 12 minutes.

Meanwhile, place the pumpkin seeds in a single layer in a heavy, dry skillet over medium-high heat. Shake or stir the seeds frequently, about 5 minutes. When seeds begin to pop, stay close to the pan and keep the seeds moving almost constantly. You want them all to pop, if possible, but do not let them get too brown. Remove from the pan, cool a bit, mince, and set aside.

Transfer the packets to warmed serving plates and instruct your guests to pinch and tear the paper to release the aromatic steam. The contents may then be lifted out onto the plate and the paper removed from the table and discarded. Serve very hot, passing the pumpkin seeds to sprinkle on top.

EACH SERVING PROVIDES:
51 calories, 2g protein, 1g fat, 2g dietary fiber
10g carbohydrate, 82mg sodium, 0mg cholesterol

Steamed Corn with Pimiento and Horseradish

ALMOST INSTANT

Fresh, sweet corn at the peak of the season is preferred for this dish, but frozen corn will suffice. Purchase 6 large ears of corn to yield 3 cups of kernels. The horseradish adds a subtle, not hot, flavor; however, you may increase the amount if you like the heat.

YIELD: 6 SIDE-DISH SERVINGS

3 cups fresh or frozen corn kernels
1 teaspoon prepared horseradish
⅛ teaspoon salt
Several grinds black pepper
1 jar (4 ounces) minced pimientos
¼ cup minced fresh parsley

PLACE the corn kernels on a steamer rack in a saucepan that has a tight-fitting lid. Add about 2 inches of water, cover, and cook over medium-high heat for 8 minutes if frozen, 10–12 minutes if fresh (cooking time will depend on the variety and sugar content of the corn; it is done when tender-crisp).

Meanwhile, mix together the horseradish, salt, pepper, and undrained pimientos in a medium-size bowl. Drain the corn and add it to the pimiento mixture. Toss to combine, then add the parsley, toss again, and serve immediately.

EACH SERVING PROVIDES:
83 calories, 3g protein, 1g fat, 3g dietary fiber
18g carbohydrate, 64mg sodium, 0mg cholesterol

PASTA DISHES

* * * * * * * * *

PASTA DISHES

Five-Minute Couscous

Simple Spaghetti Sicilian-Style

Cappellini with Tomatoes, Arugula, and Calamata Olives

Fettuccine with Zucchini, Roasted Peppers, Almonds,
    and Mint

Vermicelli with Curried Eggplant and Chard in
    Ginger Tomato Sauce

Bucatini with Green Beans, Tomatoes, and Olives

Lasagnette with Spicy Greens, Adzuki Beans, and
    Shiitake Mushrooms

Mediterranean Asparagus and Artichokes with Fusilli

Peas and Orzo with Olives, Tarragon, and Pecans

Soba Noodles with Shredded Vegetables
    and Spicy Peanut Sauce

Porcini Mushroom Stroganoff

FEW WOULD ARGUE that pasta presides among the world's favorite foods. Throughout Europe, Asia, and the Americas, some form of pasta plays an important role in every regional cuisine. It earned its prominence by combining so deliciously with so many foods. Mushrooms and garlic, vegetables and nuts, tomatoes and beans, a garden full of herbs—all can mingle happily in a bowl with strands or ribbons, bows or tubes, or tiny stars of pasta. And however we choose to prepare it, pasta is certain to satisfy.

Pasta can be formal or fun, delicate or substantial. We may labor with love over handmade noodles or quickly toss together a simple sauce in the time it takes to boil thin strands of capellini.

Because it is versatile, convenient, and delicious, we turn again and again to pasta. Here is a small sampling of our favorite dishes.

Five-Minute Couscous

Couscous is one of our favorite convenience foods. It cooks almost instantly to make a delicious side dish for stews or stir-fries.

YIELD: 4 SIDE-DISH SERVINGS

1½ cups Homemade Vegetable Stock (see NOTE)
1 teaspoon olive oil
½ teaspoon granulated garlic
⅛ teaspoon salt
Several grinds black pepper
1 cup dried couscous

BRING stock, olive oil, garlic, salt, and pepper to a boil. Stir in the couscous, cover, and immediately turn off the heat. Let stand 5 minutes, then transfer the couscous to a serving bowl, fluffing with a fork to break up any large clumps. Serve hot.

NOTE: If you do not have Homemade Vegetable Stock on hand, make some according to the directions on page 84, or dissolve ½ large low-sodium vegetable broth cube in 1½ cups of hot water.

EACH SERVING PROVIDES:
192 calories, 6g protein, 1g fat, 1g dietary fiber
38g carbohydrate, 74mg sodium, 0mg cholesterol

Simple Spaghetti Sicilian-Style

ALMOST INSTANT

The people of Sicily are so passionate about their native food
that even the local bus driver will share his favorite recipe.
This Sicilian pasta takes little time to prepare; it will accompany a wide variety of dishes or suffice as a light main course
with a salad and bread.

YIELD: 4 SIDE-DISH SERVINGS

8 ounces dried spaghetti
2 tablespoons extra-virgin olive oil
3 cloves garlic, minced
⅛ teaspoon dried red chili flakes

BRING 6–8 quarts of water to a boil in a large stockpot and cook
the pasta until al dente. Drain and transfer to a warm, large,
shallow bowl. Meanwhile, gently heat the olive oil in a small
saucepan. Add the garlic and chili flakes, and sauté for 1–2 minutes, taking care not to brown the garlic. Pour over the pasta,
using a rubber spatula to get all of the oil out of the pan. Toss to
coat and serve immediately.

EACH SERVING PROVIDES:

200 calories, 5g protein, 7g fat, 2g dietary fiber
28g carbohydrate, 1mg sodium, 0mg cholesterol

Cappellini with Tomatoes, Arugula, and Calamata Olives

ALMOST INSTANT

This dish is a nice blending of distinctive ingredients. As a variation, you could try chopped fresh spinach in place of the arugula. This delicious pasta could be served as a satisfying main course for four, with the addition of a hearty vegetable side dish and a salad to round out the meal.

YIELD: 6 SIDE-DISH SERVINGS

3 pounds fresh pear tomatoes (or 1 can [28 ounces] whole tomatoes)
2 tablespoons olive oil
2 medium cloves garlic, minced
½ teaspoon dried red chili flakes
⅔ cup chopped calamata olives
12 ounces dried cappellini
3 cups chopped arugula

BLANCH the tomatoes by immersing them in several quarts of boiling water for a minute or two. Use a slotted spoon to lift them from the pot and immediately plunge them into a basin of cold water. When the tomatoes are cool enough to handle, peel them and cut out and discard the stem ends. Cut the tomatoes in half crosswise and gently squeeze over the sink to remove the juicy seed pockets. Coarsely chop the tomatoes and set aside. Bring the blanching water back to a boil for the pasta. (Alternatively, drain the canned tomatoes, reserving the juice for another use, such as soup stock. Coarsely chop the tomatoes and set aside. Put several quarts of water on to boil for the pasta.)

Heat the olive oil over medium heat in a large, heavy-bottomed skillet. Add the garlic and chili flakes and sauté for a minute, stirring constantly. Add the tomatoes, increase the heat to medium-high, and simmer about 10 minutes, stirring frequently, until the sauce is somewhat reduced. Stir in the olives.

Meanwhile, cook the pasta in rapidly boiling water until al dente. Drain well and toss with the arugula in a warmed serving bowl. Add the tomato sauce and toss to combine. Serve immediately.

EACH SERVING PROVIDES:

332 calories, 9g protein, 11g fat, 7g dietary fiber
51g carbohydrate, 501mg sodium, 0mg cholesterol

PERFECT PASTA

For perfectly cooked pasta, use plenty of water—about 8 quarts per pound of pasta—and bring it to a rolling boil. A sprinkling of salt and a bit of oil in the water are traditional, but not essential. Separate the pasta strands as you add them to the boiling water and stir frequently during cooking. Cook the pasta uncovered until a noodle tests al dente—"to the tooth," meaning the pasta is tender but still slightly chewy. Undercooked pasta has a hard center and an unpleasant starchy taste. Overcooked, it falls apart easily and has a mushy texture.

Fettuccine with Zucchini, Roasted Peppers, Almonds, and Mint

ALMOST INSTANT

This has become a standby in our kitchens. It is made from easy-to-find ingredients and comes together quickly. Select firm, small zucchini; they will have the best flavor and texture. You may wish to roast the peppers and toast the almonds earlier in the day to save yourself the effort at mealtime.

YIELD: 4 MAIN-DISH SERVINGS

2 large red bell peppers
¼ cup slivered raw almonds
1 pound zucchini (about 3 medium)
1 medium white onion
2 tablespoons olive oil
4 cloves garlic, minced
¼ teaspoon dried red chili flakes
¼ teaspoon salt
¾ cup minced fresh mint leaves
½ cup dry white wine
3 tablespoons fresh-squeezed lemon juice
10 ounces dried fettuccine

PLACE the peppers under a preheated broiler, on a hot grill, or directly on the burner of a gas stovetop. Turn the peppers frequently until the skins are well charred and mostly black. Transfer the peppers to a plastic or paper bag, fold to close, and set aside. The steam in the bag will finish cooking the peppers. When cooled, remove them from the bag and peel off the charred skin.

Discard the stems, seeds, and white membranes, and cut the peppers into thin 1-inch strips. Set aside.

Place the almonds in a single layer in a dry, heavy-bottomed skillet over medium-high heat. Shake the pan frequently. Soon the nuts will begin to turn golden brown, emitting a wonderful roasted aroma. Immediately remove them from the pan and set aside.

Wash and dry the zucchini and cut it into $\frac{1}{4}$-inch rounds. Trim off and discard the ends of the onion, peel it, and cut it in half lengthwise. Place each half cut side down on your work surface and slice lengthwise into $\frac{1}{4}$-inch-thick slices.

In a large pot, bring several quarts of water to a boil for the pasta. Meanwhile, heat the oil in a large skillet over medium heat. Sauté the onion, garlic, and chili flakes for about 5 minutes, stirring frequently, until the onion begins to turn golden. Add the zucchini and salt, then sauté about 15 minutes over medium-high heat, stirring frequently. The vegetables should be nicely browned. Stir in the mint and bell pepper strips, then add the wine and lemon juice. Stir and sauté about 1 minute. Cover the pan, turn off the heat, and allow to stand about 5 minutes.

Meanwhile, cook the pasta in the boiling water until al dente and drain well. Toss the hot pasta with the zucchini mixture and almonds in a warmed serving bowl until well combined. Serve hot.

EACH SERVING PROVIDES:

469 calories, 13g protein, 15g fat, 6g dietary fiber
68g carbohydrate, 149mg sodium, 0mg cholesterol

Vermicelli with Curried Eggplant and Chard in Ginger Tomato Sauce

ALMOST INSTANT

Deliciously exotic-tasting, this pasta dish is a perfect balance of sweet and hot. Wait until you find really fresh eggplant and Swiss chard to try it—it makes a big difference in texture as well as taste.

YIELD: 4 MAIN-DISH SERVINGS

2 medium fresh tomatoes (about 1 pound)
1 cup diced yellow onion
2 cloves garlic, chopped
2 teaspoons grated fresh ginger
¼ teaspoon plus pinch salt
1 cup Homemade Vegetable Stock (see NOTE)
½ pound Swiss chard
1 small eggplant (¾ pound)
1 tablespoon peanut oil
½ teaspoon cumin seeds
½ teaspoon mustard seeds
½ teaspoon ground cardamom
½ teaspoon ground turmeric
3 tablespoons currants
8 ounces dried vermicelli

CUT out and discard the stems of the tomatoes. Dice the tomatoes and combine them in a blender or food processor with the onion, garlic, ginger, the ¼ teaspoon salt, and ⅓ cup of the stock. Puree to a smooth consistency and set aside.

Bring several quarts of water to a boil for the pasta. Meanwhile, carefully wash the chard; there is no need to dry it. Tear or cut the leaves into bite-size pieces and thinly slice the stems. Set aside separately. Trim off and discard the stem of the eggplant and cut it crosswise into $\frac{1}{4}$-inch slices. Cut the slices lengthwise into $\frac{1}{4}$-inch strips, and cut the strips into 1-inch lengths.

Meanwhile, heat the oil over medium heat in a large saucepan that has a tight-fitting lid. Add the cumin and mustard seeds, cardamom, and turmeric. Stir and cook the spices for about 2 minutes, then add the remaining $\frac{2}{3}$ cup of the stock and stir. Heat to the steaming stage, then stir in the eggplant, chard stems, and the pinch of salt. Immediately cover the pan tightly and cook for 5 minutes. Remove the lid and stir in the tomato sauce, chard leaves, and currants. Cover and cook 5 minutes, then remove the lid and cook, stirring frequently, 5 minutes longer.

Meanwhile, cook the pasta in the boiling water until al dente. Drain well and toss with the sauce. Serve very hot, offering cayenne for those who like very spicy food.

NOTE: If you do not have Homemade Vegetable Stock on hand, make some according to the directions on page 84, or dissolve $\frac{1}{2}$ of a large low-sodium vegetable broth cube in 1 cup of hot water.

EACH SERVING PROVIDES:
331 calories, 10g protein, 5g fat, 6g dietary fiber
63g carbohydrate, 346mg sodium, 0mg cholesterol

Bucatini with Green Beans, Tomatoes, and Olives

Bucatini are hollow strands of pasta with a distinctive texture. If you are unable to locate them at an Italian specialty food store, you may substitute another hearty pasta variety, such as rigatoni or fusilli. This dish is robust, wholesome, and delicious.

YIELD: 4 MAIN-DISH SERVINGS

¾ pound fresh green beans
1 can (28 ounces) whole tomatoes
1 tablespoon olive oil
2 cloves garlic, minced
⅛ teaspoon dried red chili flakes
⅛ teaspoon salt
¼ cup port wine
Pinch ground cloves
1 tablespoon tomato paste
2 tablespoons minced dry oil-cured black olives
12 ounces dried bucatini

SNAP off the ends of the beans and pull off any strings. Cut the beans crosswise at a slant into 1-inch lengths. Drain the tomatoes, saving their juice for another use, such as soup stock. Coarsely chop the tomatoes and set aside in a bowl.

Bring several quarts of water to a boil for the pasta. Heat the olive oil over medium heat in a large skillet and sauté the garlic and chili flakes for about 1 minute, stirring constantly, then add the beans and salt. Sauté, stirring frequently, for 3–4 minutes, then add the tomatoes, port, and cloves. Reduce the heat to low, cover, and cook 15–20 minutes, until the beans are fork-tender. Turn off the heat and stir in the tomato paste and olives.

Meanwhile, cook the pasta in the boiling water until al dente. Drain well, add to the skillet, and toss with the hot sauce. Serve immediately.

EACH SERVING PROVIDES:

444 calories, 14g protein, 7g fat, 5g dietary fiber

80g carbohydrate, 457mg sodium, 0mg cholesterol

Lasagnette with Spicy Greens, Adzuki Beans, and Shiitake Mushrooms

Adzukis are tiny, red, protein-packed beans from the Orient. They are available in most Asian markets and natural food stores. For a Far East feast, begin the meal with a very simple miso broth and end with tea and almond cookies.

YIELD: 8 MAIN-DISH SERVINGS

1 cup dried adzuki beans
1 teaspoon dried red chili flakes
2 bay leaves
1 ounce dried shiitake mushrooms
1½ pounds mustard greens (about 2 bunches)
2 tablespoons dark sesame oil
3 medium cloves garlic, minced
1 medium yellow onion, diced
2 tablespoons grated fresh ginger
2 tablespoons soy sauce
1 pound dried lasagnette

SOAK the beans several hours or overnight. Drain and cover with fresh water in a large stockpot. Add the chili flakes and bay leaves. Bring to a boil and cook about 40 minutes, adding water occasionally as needed. Beans should be tender but not so soft they break apart easily. Drain the beans, remove the bay leaves, and set aside.

Meanwhile, soak the mushrooms in 2 cups of hot water for about 30 minutes. Lift them out of the water, reserving the soaking liquid, and wash carefully under a thin stream of running water to remove any grit in the membranes. Remove and discard the tough stems and sliver the caps. Strain the soaking liquid through a paper coffee filter into a bowl. You will have about 1½ cups, which you will use in the sauce. Set aside.

Bring several quarts of water to a boil for the pasta. Meanwhile, wash the greens carefully, discard the thick part of the stems, and chop coarsely. In a high-walled skillet or stockpot, heat the oil over medium heat and sauté the garlic and onion about 5 minutes, until the onion begins to get limp. Add the beans, mushrooms, ginger, and soy sauce, and stir and sauté 5 minutes longer. Add the greens and the mushroom soaking liquid and increase heat to medium-high. Toss and stir often as the greens wilt and most of the liquid evaporates, about 10 minutes.

Meanwhile, cook the pasta in the boiling water until al dente. Drain well and gently combine with the sauce in a warm serving bowl. Pass the pepper grinder and additional soy sauce, if desired.

EACH SERVING PROVIDES:

363 calories, 15g protein, 5g fat, 8g dietary fiber
67g carbohydrate, 284mg sodium, 0mg cholesterol

FUSION CUISINE

All the world's great culinary traditions have their signature ingredients and techniques. One of the joys of creative cooking is transcending boundaries to invent exciting international combinations. Here, a traditional Italian pasta—*mafalda*, also sold as lasagnette—is sauced with Japanese ingredients and seasonings. The result is unconventional and delicious.

Mediterranean Asparagus and Artichokes with Fusilli

ALMOST INSTANT

This was inspired by a day in April when glorious sunshine fooled us into thinking it was summer. We began to dream of the Mediterranean Sea and invented this dish to take us there in spirit.

YIELD: 6 MAIN-DISH SERVINGS

½ cup slivered dried tomatoes (see NOTE)
1½ pounds asparagus
2 jars (6 ounces each) marinated artichoke hearts
2 tablespoons olive oil
1 medium yellow onion, coarsely chopped
4 medium cloves garlic, minced
2 teaspoons dried oregano
2 teaspoons dried spearmint
¼ teaspoon salt
A few grinds black pepper
¾ cup dry white wine
1 pound dried fusilli
¼ cup minced fresh parsley leaves

PUT several quarts of water on to boil for the pasta. Break off the tough stem ends of the asparagus and cut at a slant into 1-inch pieces. Drain the artichoke hearts, reserving the liquid for another use. Heat 1 tablespoon of the olive oil over medium heat in a large skillet. Sauté the onion and garlic with the oregano and spearmint 5 minutes, until the onion is golden and limp. Add the asparagus, salt, and pepper; stir and sauté 5 minutes. Add the artichoke hearts and dried tomatoes; stir and sauté about 5 minutes longer. Stir the wine into the asparagus mixture and continue to cook about 5 minutes. Meanwhile, cook the pasta until al dente. Drain well. In a warm serving bowl, toss the hot pasta with the remaining 1 tablespoon olive oil. Toss again with the vegetable mixture. Sprinkle with the parsley and serve.

NOTE: If the dried tomatoes are too dry to sliver, soak them in hot water 15–30 minutes. Drain the tomatoes well and sliver them.

EACH SERVING PROVIDES:

474 calories, 13g protein, 16g fat, 7g dietary fiber

68g carbohydrate, 365mg sodium, 0mg cholesterol

Peas and Orzo with Olives, Tarragon, and Pecans

ALMOST INSTANT

Here is another comfort food creation. It comes together very quickly and you'll find yourself making it frequently from ingredients you will want to keep on hand. Orzo, the rice-shaped pasta of Greek cuisine, is available at any market with a good pasta selection. Oil-cured olives are actually packaged dry, not in a brine. A well-stocked deli counter or gourmet food store will have them.

YIELD: 6 SIDE-DISH SERVINGS

Pinch salt
2 tablespoons fresh-squeezed lemon juice
2 tablespoons minced, dry oil-cured black olives
1 tablespoon minced fresh tarragon leaves
1 clove garlic, minced
Several grinds black pepper
3 tablespoons chopped raw unsalted pecans
1 cup dried orzo
1 pound frozen petite peas
2 teaspoons olive oil
6 fresh lemon wedges

BRING 6 cups of water to a boil in a large saucepan with the salt. Meanwhile, in a small bowl, combine the lemon juice, olives, tarragon, garlic, and pepper and set aside at room temperature. Place the pecans in a single layer in a dry, heavy-bottomed skillet over medium-high heat and cook, stirring frequently, for several minutes, until nuts are browning and emit a wonderful roasted aroma. Remove them from the pan and set aside.

Cook the orzo in salted boiling water for about 10 minutes, until it is al dente, then add the frozen peas. As soon as the water comes back to a boil, transfer the orzo and peas to a colander and drain very well. In a warmed serving bowl, toss the orzo and peas with the olive oil until well combined, then with the olive mixture and the pecans. Garnish with lemon wedges and serve hot or at room temperature.

EACH SERVING PROVIDES:

222 calories, 8g protein, 6g fat, 4g dietary fiber

35g carbohydrate, 225mg sodium, 0mg cholesterol

Soba Noodles with Shredded Vegetables and Spicy Peanut Sauce

Soba noodles get their distinctive flavor from buckwheat flour. You can purchase them at Asian markets or natural-food stores. Take your time cutting the vegetables very thinly; from that point on the preparation is quite simple.

YIELD: 4 MAIN-DISH SERVINGS

1 medium carrot
¼ pound snow peas, strings removed
½ pound button mushrooms, very thinly sliced
½ cup vegetable stock or water
3 tablespoons creamy peanut butter
2 tablespoons rice wine vinegar
1 tablespoon brown rice syrup
2 teaspoons grated fresh ginger
2 cloves garlic, minced
2 teaspoons soy sauce
¼ teaspoon cayenne
10 ounces dried buckwheat soba noodles
1 tablespoon dark sesame oil
2 tablespoons dry sherry
1 small yellow onion, finely diced
2 cups finely shredded green or Napa cabbage
1 cup fresh mung bean or soybean sprouts
4 lime wedges

CUT the carrot into matchsticks. Slice the snow peas length-wise into thin slivers.

For the peanut sauce, whisk together the stock, peanut butter, vinegar, rice syrup, ginger, garlic, soy sauce, and cayenne until well combined. Set aside.

Bring about 12 cups of water to a boil in a large pot. Add the soba noodles and stir to separate. As soon as the water returns to a rolling boil, add 1 cup of cold water. Return to boiling, then immediately turn off the heat and leave the noodles in the hot water for 5 minutes. Drain well, without rinsing.

Heat the oil and sherry in a wok or heavy-bottomed skillet over medium-high heat. Add the onion and stir-fry for 2 minutes. Add the carrot, snow peas, cabbage, mushrooms, and salt. Stir-fry for 4–5 minutes, until the vegetables have begun to wilt. Add the peanut sauce and cook about 1 minute, until bubbling. Add the noodles and toss gently, until well combined with sauce and vegetables. Add another few tablespoons of stock if the mixture seems too dry.

Divide among four heated serving bowls and top each serving with a quarter of the sprouts. Nestle a lime wedge into each bowl and serve immediately.

EACH SERVING PROVIDES:
442 calories, 18g protein, 11g fat, 7g dietary fiber
76g carbohydrate, 817mg sodium, 0mg cholesterol

Porcini Mushroom Stroganoff

The porcini mushrooms give this vegan version of stroganoff a rich, full flavor. The soy milk creates a satisfying creamy texture. This will become a standby family favorite.

YIELD: 4 MAIN-DISH SERVINGS

½ ounce dried porcini mushrooms
1 pound button mushrooms
1 tablespoon olive oil
1 small yellow onion, chopped
2 cloves garlic, minced
12 ounces dried fettuccine
2 tablespoons unbleached flour
2 tablespoons dry white wine
1 tablespoon tomato paste
¾ cup plain soy milk

POUR 1 cup of very hot water over the porcini mushrooms in a small bowl. Cover and steep for 30 minutes. Meanwhile, brush or wipe the button mushrooms clean and trim off the stem ends. Thinly slice and set aside. Heat the olive oil in a large skillet over medium heat and add the onion and garlic. Sauté about a minute, then add the button mushrooms. Cover the skillet and sauté for 20 minutes, stirring occasionally, until the mushrooms release their liquid.

Meanwhile, preheat the oven to 350 degrees F. and bring several quarts of water to a boil for the pasta. Lift the porcini mushrooms from their soaking liquid and set them aside, reserving the liquid. Strain the liquid through a paper coffee filter and set it aside. Chop the porcinis and add them to the mushrooms in the skillet. Stir to combine, and continue to cook, uncovered, over medium heat about 5 minutes. Cook the pasta until al dente while you finish the sauce.

Place about ¼ cup of the reserved mushroom soaking liquid in a small jar that has a tight-fitting lid. Add the flour and shake to dissolve. Stir this into the skillet along with the remaining mushroom soaking liquid, wine, and tomato paste. Continue to cook until the sauce thickens, stirring frequently, about 5 minutes. Stir in the soy milk and continue to cook for another minute or two.

Drain the pasta and transfer it to a warmed serving bowl. Spoon the mushroom mixture over the top and serve immediately.

EACH SERVING PROVIDES:

413 calories, 15g protein, 6g fat, 7g dietary fiber
75g carbohydrate, 59mg sodium, 0mg cholesterol

ELEGANT FIRESIDE DINNER

•••

Red Lentil Pâté with Tarragon, page 10

Porcini Mushroom Stroganoff, page 134

Sherry-Sautéed Broccoli with Fresh Thyme, page 100

Mixed greens with red wine vinaigrette

Sonoma County Merlot

GRAIN DISHES

GRAIN DISHES

Italian-Style Wild Rice and Vegetables

Spicy Black-Eyed Peas and Rice

Mushroom Quinoa Pilaf

Carrot, Kasha, and Caraway Pilaf

Beets and Greens with Bulgur and Miso Tahini Sauce

Acorn Squash Stuffed with Bulgur, Celery Seeds,
    and Shiitake Mushrooms

Soft Polenta with Corn Kernels and Sage

Tri-Color Pepper Sauté over Grilled Polenta

Grilled Winter Squash with Millet Pilaf and
    Coconut Chutney Sauce

Risotto with Winter Vegetables and Fresh Sage

Risotto with Fresh Fennel and Carrots

Asparagus Risotto with Oyster Mushrooms and Ginger

Baked Millet and Sweet Potato Patties with
    Spinach and Cilantro Sauce

Quinoa, Rice, and French Lentil Timbales with
    Roasted Red Pepper Sauce

F OR SHEER EARTHY GOODNESS and hearty sustenance, nothing outshines grains. A creamy risotto laced with herbs; a steaming, vegetable-studded pilaf; grilled polenta with a savory topping—these are the wholesome, delicious foods we frequently crave.

Nutritionally, whole grains are powerhouses and deserve star billing in our diets. Rice is a traditional favorite, but the realm of grains is vast. In this chapter, we provide a sampling of the lesser-known varieties, such as quinoa and kasha, which are distinctive and delicious, and bring welcome diversity to everyday cooking.

A pantry stocked with a large selection of dried grains is a source of creative inspiration as well as nourishment. Let these new and different grain dishes, suitable as dinner accompaniments or as meals unto themselves, expand your culinary possibilities.

Italian-Style Wild Rice and Vegetables

Rice and vegetables have been a mainstay in the vegetarian diet for years. This version uses traditional Italian seasonings, but the wild rice lends a new twist.

YIELD: 4 SIDE-DISH SERVINGS

The rice
1 tablespoon olive oil
¾ cup uncooked long-grain brown rice
¼ cup uncooked wild rice
1 teaspoon dried basil
1 teaspoon dried oregano

The vegetables
2 tablespoons olive oil
3 cloves garlic, minced
1 can (28 ounces) diced tomatoes
1 cup chopped broccoli
1 cup chopped cauliflower
1 cup sliced green beans
1 teaspoon dried oregano
1 teaspoon dried basil
1 tablespoon capers, drained

PUT 1 tablespoon of oil in a 2-quart pan over low heat and add both rices along with the basil and oregano. Sauté for a minute, stirring constantly. Add 2½ cups of water, bring to a boil, cover, reduce heat to low, and simmer 45–50 minutes until the water is absorbed and rice is tender.

Meanwhile, heat 2 tablespoons of oil in a skillet that has a tight-fitting lid. Sauté the garlic over medium heat 1 minute, then add the tomatoes and their juice. Add all of the vegetables and the herbs. Bring to a rapid simmer over medium-high heat, cover, and cook for 15 minutes. Uncover and cook 10 minutes longer to reduce the liquid. Vegetables should be tender but not overly soft. Mound the rice on a large serving platter and top with the vegetables. Sprinkle with the capers and serve immediately.

EACH SERVING PROVIDES:

291 calories, 8g protein, 12g fat, 6g dietary fiber

42g carbohydrate, 99mg sodium, 0mg cholesterol

Spicy Black-Eyed Peas and Rice

Here is a simple and delicious vegan version of Hoppin'
John, the classic Southern side dish typically flavored with
salt pork. The onions are long and slowly sautéed to bring
out a mellow, caramelized flavor. Be sure to season the dish
with plenty of black pepper for an authentic touch. Serve this
alongside any Mexican or Southwestern stew or stir-fry.

YIELD: 8 SIDE-DISH SERVINGS

1½ cups uncooked long-grain brown rice
1 bay leaf
½ teaspoon salt
2 tablespoons olive oil
2 medium white onions, diced
Several grinds black pepper
2 cups freshly cooked or canned black-eyed peas, drained
½ cup pea cooking liquid or vegetable stock
Several drops hot pepper sauce

BRING 3 cups of water to a boil and stir in the rice, bay leaf,
and ¼ teaspoon of the salt. Return to a boil, reduce heat to
very low, cover, and simmer 40–50 minutes, until the water has
been absorbed and the rice is tender. Remove the bay leaf.

Meanwhile, heat the olive oil in a heavy-bottomed skillet over
medium heat. Add the onions, the remaining ¼ teaspoon salt,
and pepper. Sauté, stirring frequently, 15–20 minutes, until
onions are very soft and well browned. If onions seem to be
browning too rapidly, reduce the heat and stir more frequently.

Heat the cooked peas and the ½ cup cooking liquid in a large pan or Dutch oven over medium heat. When they are hot, stir in the onions. Add the cooked rice and more pepper to taste; typically, Southern cooks would use a lot. Stir in the hot pepper sauce. Serve immediately.

EACH SERVING PROVIDES:

175 calories, 6g protein, 4g fat, 6g dietary fiber
29g carbohydrate, 150mg sodium, 0mg cholesterol

A SPICY AUTUMN FEAST

Potato, Zucchini, and Olive Stew with Garlic,
Jalapeños, and Tomatoes, page 78

Spicy Black-Eyed Peas and Rice, page 142

Spinach salad with cumin-orange vinaigrette

Fresh lemonade or chilled dark beer

Mushroom Quinoa Pilaf

Here is an elegant pilaf starring a grain with humble origins.
Quinoa dates back to the time of the Incas. It has been
reintroduced for modern times as one of the plant realm's
high quality protein foods, providing all of the essential
amino acids. Quinoa is available in natural-food stores and
other specialty markets. Because it is so nutritious and satisfying, we enjoy this pilaf as a main dish, accompanied by salad
and steamed vegetables. It would also serve as a very special
side dish for 6 to 8 people.

YIELD: 4 MAIN-DISH SERVINGS

½ cup slivered raw almonds
1 ounce dried porcini mushrooms
½ pound button mushrooms
1 tablespoon olive oil
2 tablespoons dry sherry
2 cloves garlic, minced
1 medium yellow onion, chopped
1 medium red bell pepper, chopped
1 teaspoon dried marjoram
1 cup uncooked quinoa

PLACE the almonds in a dry, heavy-bottomed skillet over
medium-high heat. Stir them frequently as they toast. When
they are golden brown in color, immediately remove them from
the pan and set aside.

Pour 2 cups of hot water over the porcini mushrooms in a
bowl. Cover and steep for 30 minutes. Lift the porcini mushrooms from their soaking liquid, reserving the liquid. Chop the
porcini mushrooms and set aside. Strain the liquid through a
paper coffee filter and set it aside.

Brush or wipe the button mushrooms clean and trim off the stem ends. Thinly slice the mushrooms and set aside. Heat the olive oil and sherry in a large skillet over medium heat and add the garlic, onion, and bell pepper. Sauté for about 2 minutes, stirring occasionally, then add the marjoram and button mushrooms. Stir to combine, then cover the skillet and cook for about 10 minutes, until the mushrooms release their liquid. Add the porcini mushrooms to the skillet and continue to sauté for 5 minutes. Stir occasionally.

Meanwhile, place the quinoa in a bowl in the sink and thoroughly rinse it by rubbing the grains together with your hands. Drain it thoroughly in a strainer. Measure the reserved mushroom soaking liquid and add additional water to yield 2 cups. Place this stock in a pan over high heat and bring to a boil. Add the quinoa, cover, and reduce heat to low. Simmer about 15 minutes, until all the water has been absorbed and the grain is tender.

Stir the quinoa into the mushroom mixture and continue to cook for about 2 minutes. Place the pilaf on a platter and top with the toasted almonds. Serve immediately.

EACH SERVING PROVIDES:

373 calories, 11g protein, 17g fat, 6g dietary fiber

47g carbohydrate, 10mg sodium, 0mg cholesterol

Carrot, Kasha, and Caraway Pilaf

The flavor and aroma of kasha are earthy, nutty, and quite distinctive—almost impossible to describe. Its texture is hearty and chewy, not delicate. Here it is combined with some classic seasonings of eastern Europe and Russia, where kasha is well loved. Small amounts of leftover pilaf can be added to salads and soups for a distinctive flavor and texture note.

YIELD: 6 SIDE-DISH SERVINGS

1 tablespoon canola oil
1 medium carrot, diced small
½ medium yellow onion, diced
1 cup whole roasted buckwheat groats (kasha)
2 cloves garlic, minced
1 teaspoon caraway seeds, crushed
2 cups Homemade Vegetable Stock (see NOTE)
¼ teaspoon salt
Several grinds black pepper
2 teaspoons sweet paprika

HEAT the oil over medium heat in a heavy-bottomed skillet or Dutch oven that has a tight-fitting lid. Add the carrot and onion and sauté 5 minutes. Add the kasha, garlic, and caraway and sauté 3 minutes. Stir in the stock, salt, and pepper. Bring to a simmer, cover the pan tightly, reduce the heat to low, and cook 20 minutes. Turn off the heat and allow to stand 10 minutes before removing the lid. Transfer the kasha to a bowl or platter and toss with the paprika, breaking up large clumps as you do. Serve hot.

NOTE: If you do not have Homemade Vegetable Stock on hand, make some according to the directions on page 84, or dissolve ½ of a large low-sodium vegetable broth cube in 2 cups of hot water.

EACH SERVING PROVIDES:
136 calories, 4g protein, 3g fat, 4g dietary fiber
250g carbohydrate, 158mg sodium, 0mg cholesterol

Beets and Greens with Bulgur and Miso Tahini Sauce

This dish is scrumptious and wholesome. The preparation has several steps, but once you make it, you will realize how simple a meal it is. If you wish, you may serve the beets as a side dish without the bulgur. In that case, you will need less of the sauce, but the remainder will keep well in the refrigerator.

YIELD: 6 MAIN-DISH SERVINGS

2 pounds beets, with greens (about 8 medium)
1½ cups uncooked bulgur wheat
Pinch salt
Several grinds black pepper
4 green onions, minced
2 tablespoons toasted sesame tahini
3 tablespoons light-colored miso
3 tablespoons fresh-squeezed lemon juice
1 clove garlic, minced
Pinch cayenne

TRIM the greens from the beets, leaving about ½ inch of stems attached to the roots. Set the greens aside. Rinse the beets and place them on a steamer rack in a saucepan that has a tight-fitting lid. Add about 2 inches of water, cover the pan, and cook over medium-high heat about 25 minutes, until each beet can be easily pierced all the way through with a sharp knife (cooking time will vary, depending on the size of the beet). Remove the lid to check the water level midway through the cooking time and add additional hot water, if necessary. When they are tender, remove the cooked beets from the pan and set them aside.

Meanwhile, place the bulgur in a medium saucepan over high heat and stir and roast about 2 minutes. Stir in 3 cups of water, salt, pepper, and green onions. Bring to a boil over high heat, reduce heat to very low, cover the pan, and cook 15 minutes. Allow to stand, covered, 5 minutes and fluff with a fork before serving.

Meanwhile, in a small bowl, mash the tahini and miso together with a fork until well combined. Add the lemon juice and mash some more until incorporated. Add ⅓ cup hot water a little at a time, stirring to incorporate after each addition. When all the water has been added, whisk to create a smooth consistency. Stir in the garlic and cayenne and set aside in a warm place.

Wash the beet greens, removing the tough stems. Tear the greens into bite-size pieces. Do not dry them—the water that clings to the leaves will provide the liquid for steaming. Pile the leaves into a saucepan, cover, and cook over medium heat 5 minutes, until they are wilted. Drain in a colander, using the back of a wooden spoon to press out as much water as possible. Keep warm.

When the beets are just cool enough to handle, slip the skins off. Slice the beets into ¼-inch rounds.

To serve, mound the hot bulgur in the center of a platter. Arrange the sliced beets and their greens around the outside in a pretty pattern. Drizzle the sauce slowly over everything to distribute it evenly. Garnish with additional minced green onions, if you wish, and serve warm or at room temperature.

EACH SERVING PROVIDES:
217 calories, 9g protein, 4g fat, 10g dietary fiber
41g carbohydrate, 636mg sodium, 0mg cholesterol

Acorn Squash Stuffed with Bulgur, Celery Seeds, and Shiitake Mushrooms

This early autumn vegetable deserves an appearance on your dinner table. Other varieties of winter squash, such as hubbard or butternut, are also enjoyable prepared this way.

YIELD: 4 MAIN-DISH SERVINGS

½ ounce dried shiitake mushrooms
1 tablespoon canola oil
2 cloves garlic, minced
½ teaspoon celery seeds, crushed
¼ teaspoon salt
½ cup uncooked bulgur wheat
6 ounces silken tofu, mashed with a fork
2 green onions, minced
1 tablespoon balsamic vinegar
2 medium acorn squashes

SOAK the mushrooms in 1¼ cups hot water for 30 minutes. Lift them out and strain the liquid through cheesecloth or a coffee filter, reserving the liquid. Carefully wash the mushrooms under a thin stream of water to remove any particles of dirt that may be lodged in the membranes. Gently squeeze the mushrooms to remove excess water. Discard the tough stems; chop the caps and set aside.

Bring the reserved mushroom soaking liquid to a boil in a medium-size saucepan and add the oil, garlic, celery seeds, and salt. Stir in the bulgur, cover, and immediately turn off the heat. Let sit, without disturbing the lid, for 15 minutes.

Preheat the oven to 350 degrees F. Fluff the cooked bulgur with a fork, then stir in the mushrooms, tofu, green onions, and vinegar. Cut the squashes in half lengthwise. Scoop out and discard the seeds. Spoon a quarter of the bulgur mixture into each half, then carefully place the squashes in a glass baking dish. Add hot water to the dish to a depth of about 1 inch. Bake, covered, for 50 minutes, or until the squash is tender.

EACH SERVING PROVIDES:

231 calories, 8g protein, 7g fat, 9g dietary fiber

39g carbohydrate, 145mg sodium, 0mg cholesterol

Soft Polenta with Corn Kernels and Sage

This soft-style polenta is a wonderful companion dish to grilled vegetables. The corn kernels give the polenta a nice crunch and the fresh sage provides a delightful flavor. If you are using fresh corn, purchase 2 large ears to yield 1 cup of kernels.

YIELD: 6 SIDE-DISH SERVINGS

1 tablespoon olive oil
1 tablespoon mirin
1 medium yellow onion, minced
2 cloves garlic, minced
1 cup fresh or frozen corn kernels
¼ cup minced fresh sage
6 cups water
¾ teaspoon salt
1½ cups yellow cornmeal (polenta)

HEAT the oil and mirin together in a skillet over medium-high heat and add the onion and garlic. Sauté for about 5 minutes, stirring occasionally, until the onions have begun to soften. Add the corn kernels and cook, stirring frequently, until slightly charred, about 12 minutes. Stir in the sage and continue to cook for 1–2 minutes, then remove the pan from the heat.

Combine the water and salt in a large saucepan and bring to a boil over high heat. Gradually pour in the cornmeal in a slow, steady stream, whisking constantly. Reduce the heat to medium-low and gently simmer about 20 minutes, stirring almost constantly with a wooden spoon. The polenta will thicken as it cooks. When it is thick enough to pull away from the sides of the pan, it is done. Stir in the onion-corn mixture and serve immediately.

EACH SERVING PROVIDES:

171 calories, 4g protein, 4g fat, 6g dietary fiber

34g carbohydrate, 285mg sodium, 0mg cholesterol

SUMMER HARVEST FEAST

Crostini with Greek Eggplant Topping, page 22

Soft Polenta with Fresh Corn Kernels and Sage, page 152

Green Beans with Watercress and Orange Mint Dressing, page 36

Sauvignon Blanc or iced herbal tea

Tri-Color Pepper Sauté Over Grilled Polenta

We especially enjoy this dish in the late summer when peppers are abundant. Serve it as an appetizer to begin a Mediterranean-inspired dinner party or as a light supper accompanied by a salad.

YIELD: 4 MAIN-DISH SERVINGS

The polenta
1 teaspoon dried oregano
1 teaspoon salt
1 cup yellow cornmeal (polenta)
2 tablespoons olive oil

The sauté
1 large red bell pepper
1 large yellow bell pepper
1 large green bell pepper
1 large yellow onion
2 tablespoons olive oil
3 cloves garlic, minced
1 teaspoon dried oregano
1 tablespoon balsamic vinegar

HEAT 4 cups of water to a simmer over medium-high heat in a heavy-bottomed saucepan. Crush 1 teaspoon oregano with a mortar and pestle to a fine consistency, or crush thoroughly with your fingers, then add to the water along with the salt. Pour in the cornmeal in a slow, steady stream, whisking constantly. Reduce the heat to medium-low and gently simmer about 20 minutes, stirring almost constantly with a wooden spoon. As it cooks, the polenta will thicken. When it is thick enough to pull away from the sides of the pan, the polenta is done. Stir in 2 tablespoons of olive oil. Pour the hot cooked polenta into a loaf pan, cover with plastic wrap so it does not dry out, and allow it to cool at room temperature for at least 1 hour, or refrigerate for up to 2 days.

Cut the peppers in half and remove the stems, seeds, and white membranes. Slice the peppers lengthwise into thin strips. Peel the onion, cut it in half lengthwise, and cut each half into ¼-inch slices. Heat 2 tablespoons olive oil in a large skillet over medium heat and add the garlic. Sauté for about a minute, then stir in the onion, peppers, and 1 teaspoon oregano. Continue to sauté for 30 minutes, until the peppers and onion are tender. Add the balsamic vinegar and stir to coat. Set aside in a warm spot.

Meanwhile, preheat a coal or gas grill to medium-high. Cut the cooled polenta loaf into slices about ¾ inch thick. Lightly brush or spray the grill with olive oil and place the polenta slices on the grill. Cook for 5–6 minutes, then turn and cook another 2–3 minutes.

Arrange the grilled polenta on a large serving platter or on individual serving plates. Top with the peppers and serve immediately.

EACH SERVING PROVIDES:

299 calories, 5g protein, 14g fat, 4g dietary fiber

39g carbohydrate, 545mg sodium, 0mg cholesterol

Grilled Winter Squash with Millet Pilaf and Coconut Chutney Sauce

Here is a delicious and delicate blending of some classic flavors from India and Thailand. Despite the several steps, it is simple to make. Serve a leafy salad and crisp crackers with hummus on the side for an exotic feast your guests won't soon forget.

YIELD: 4 MAIN-DISH SERVINGS

½ cup coconut milk
⅓ cup prepared mango chutney
1 tablespoon fresh-squeezed lime juice
⅔ cup uncooked millet
1½ cups Homemade Vegetable Stock (see NOTE)
2 medium acorn or delicata squashes (about 1 pound each)
4 teaspoons canola oil
1 small yellow onion, diced small
1 small carrot, diced small
2 cloves garlic, minced
1 teaspoon mustard seeds, crushed
1 teaspoon cumin seeds, crushed
1 teaspoon fennel seeds, crushed
4 cups loosely packed, finely chopped napa cabbage
⅛ teaspoon salt
⅛ teaspoon cayenne

To make the sauce, combine the coconut milk, chutney, and lime juice in a food processor or blender and puree until smooth. Set aside at room temperature so the flavors can blend. Preheat a coal or gas grill to medium-high.

Rinse and drain the millet and toast it in a dry, heavy-bottomed skillet over medium-low heat for 5 minutes, stirring constantly. Meanwhile, bring the stock to a boil in a saucepan. Add the toasted millet to the hot stock. Cover the pot, reduce heat to low, and simmer 25 minutes. Turn off the heat and allow the pot to sit with lid undisturbed until you are ready for the millet.

Meanwhile, cut the squashes in half lengthwise. Do not peel them. Scrape out and discard the seeds. Slice each half into 1-inch wedges. Use 2 teaspoons of the oil to lightly coat both sides of each squash wedge. Place the squash on the hot grill and cook about 3–4 minutes per side, turning once. Squash should be quite tender but not falling apart.

Heat the remaining 2 teaspoons of oil over medium heat in a sauté pan or skillet. Add the onion, carrot, and garlic, along with the mustard, cumin, and fennel seeds. Sauté, stirring frequently, 5 minutes. Add the cabbage, salt, and cayenne and sauté 5 minutes longer, until cabbage is wilted. Gently, but thoroughly, combine the sautéed vegetables with the hot cooked millet.

Mound the hot pilaf onto individual serving plates. Arrange grilled squash wedges alongside each portion of pilaf. Spoon the sauce generously over the squash and serve immediately.

NOTE: If you do not have Homemade Vegetable Stock on hand, make some according to the directions on page 84, or dissolve ½ large low-sodium vegetable broth cube in 1½ cups of hot water.

EACH SERVING PROVIDES:
362 calories, 8g protein, 14g fat, 9g dietary fiber
56g carbohydrate, 165mg sodium, 0mg cholesterol

Risotto with Winter Vegetables and Fresh Sage

This risotto has an earthy quality. The root vegetables combine wonderfully with the sage. Serve this as a main dish with a salad and bread, or as a first course or side dish for 6 as part of a multicourse meal.

YIELD: 4 MAIN-DISH SERVINGS

3½ cups Homemade Vegetable Stock (see NOTE)
1 large leek (about ½ pound)
1 can (16 ounces) whole pear tomatoes
2 tablespoons olive oil
2 cloves garlic, minced
1 medium carrot, diced
1 medium turnip, diced
½ cup dry red wine
1 cup uncooked arborio rice
2 tablespoons minced fresh sage leaves
¼ teaspoon salt
Several grinds black pepper

HEAT the stock in a saucepan until just steaming and keep handy near the stove. Cut off and discard the tough green tops from the leek. Slice the leek in half lengthwise and carefully wash away any sand or dirt caught in the layers. Dice and set aside.

Drain the juice from the can of tomatoes into a bowl. Coarsely chop the tomatoes into another bowl. Set aside.

Heat the oil in a large skillet over medium heat. Sauté the garlic and leek for about 5 minutes, then add the reserved tomato juice and ½ cup of water. Stir in the carrot and turnip, cover, and cook for about 25 minutes until the vegetables are fork-tender.

Stir occasionally during the cooking time to ensure that they do not stick to the bottom of the pan.

Meanwhile, place the wine in a large, heavy-bottomed saucepan. Heat over medium heat until steaming and stir in the rice. Cook, stirring constantly, until the wine is almost completely absorbed. Add ½ cup of the stock at a time, stirring almost constantly and waiting until the liquid is almost completely absorbed before each addition. Add the sage, salt, pepper, chopped tomatoes, and cooked vegetables with the last ½ cup of stock. When the last addition of stock has been absorbed and the rice is creamy and tender, serve immediately.

NOTE: If you do not have Homemade Vegetable Stock on hand, make some according to the directions on page 84, or dissolve 1 large low-sodium vegetable broth cube in 3½ cups of hot water.

EACH SERVING PROVIDES:
329 calories, 5g protein, 8g fat, 2g dietary fiber
58g carbohydrate, 525mg sodium, 0mg cholesterol

Risotto with Fresh Fennel and Carrots

The essence of Italian country cooking is expressed in this simple risotto dish. The vegetables of midwinter are wrapped up in warm, creamy rice. Fennel is a member of the parsley family that looks similar to celery and has a pronounced licorice flavor.

YIELD: 4 MAIN-DISH SERVINGS

3½ cups Homemade Vegetable Stock (see NOTE)
2 tablespoons brandy
1½ cups diced fresh fennel bulb (about 1 large)
1 medium carrot, diced
½ cup chopped yellow onion
2 tablespoons olive oil
1 cup uncooked arborio rice
1 teaspoon dried basil
¼ cup minced fresh Italian parsley leaves

HEAT the stock in a saucepan until just steaming and keep handy near the stove. Place the brandy and 2 tablespoons of the stock in a 2-quart pot that has a tight-fitting lid over medium heat. Add the fennel, carrot, and onion. Stir to coat, cover, and cook for 10 minutes, removing the lid occasionally to stir the vegetables around. When the vegetables are fork-tender, uncover the pan and turn off the heat.

Meanwhile, heat the oil in a heavy-bottomed saucepan over medium heat and add the rice. Stir to coat the rice with the oil, then add about ½ cup of the stock and the basil, and stir constantly until the liquid is almost completely absorbed. Add the remaining stock ½ cup at a time, stirring almost constantly and waiting until the liquid is almost completely absorbed before each addition. Add the braised vegetables and parsley with the last ½ cup of stock. When the last addition of stock has been absorbed and the rice is creamy and tender, transfer to a warmed serving bowl. Garnish with parsley or fennel sprigs.

NOTE: If you do not have Homemade Vegetable Stock on hand, make some according to the directions on page 84, or dissolve 1 large low-sodium vegetable broth cube in 3½ cups of hot water.

EACH SERVING PROVIDES:

297 calories, 4g protein, 7g fat, 2g dietary fiber
51g carbohydrate, 188mg sodium, 0mg cholesterol

ARBORIO RICE

Northern Italians grow delicious specialty rices and have developed an inspired repertoire of rice preparations, the most famous of which is risotto. Risotto dishes call for an oval, short-grain rice—most notably *fino arborio*—that releases its starch gradually during the cooking process to create a creamy texture. Don't rinse arborio rice before cooking as you don't want to wash away any of this starch. Because of arborio's unique characteristics, there is no appropriate substitute. Fortunately, this wonderful rice is now widely available.

Asparagus Risotto with Oyster Mushrooms and Ginger

A true comfort food, risotto is a good choice for evenings when appetites are strong. This stunning asparagus and mushroom version would be the perfect meal after a day of working in the spring garden.

YIELD: 6 MAIN-DISH SERVINGS

5½ cups Homemade Vegetable Stock (see NOTE)
1 tablespoon low-sodium soy sauce
1 tablespoon grated fresh ginger
1 pound fresh asparagus
6 ounces fresh oyster mushrooms
2 teaspoons dark sesame oil
4 cloves garlic, minced
¼ teaspoon dried red chili flakes
½ medium red bell pepper, diced
⅛ teaspoon salt
¼ cup dry sherry
2 teaspoons olive oil
1½ cups uncooked arborio rice
3 minced green onions

HEAT the stock, soy sauce, and ginger in a saucepan until just steaming, and keep this broth handy near the stove. Rinse the asparagus, break off and discard the tough stem ends, and cut at a slant into 1-inch pieces. Rinse the mushrooms, pat dry, and chop coarsely.

In a large heavy-bottomed saucepan, heat the sesame oil over medium heat. Add half of the garlic and the red chili flakes and sauté a minute or two, stirring constantly. Add the bell pepper, asparagus, and salt. Sauté 5 minutes, stirring frequently. Stir in the mushrooms, add the sherry, and immediately cover the pan tightly. Remove the pan from the heat and set aside with the lid on.

In a large, heavy-bottomed saucepan, heat the olive oil over medium heat. Sauté the remaining garlic for 1 minute, then add the rice and stir to coat with the oil and garlic. Add 1 cup of broth to the rice, and stir gently until the liquid is absorbed. Add the remaining broth ½ cup at a time, stirring almost constantly and waiting until liquid is absorbed before each addition. When the last addition of broth has been absorbed and the rice is creamy and tender, stir in the asparagus and mushrooms, along with any pan juices. Heat through for 1 minute. Transfer to a warmed tureen or individual serving bowls and sprinkle with the green onions. Serve very hot.

NOTE: If you do not have Homemade Vegetable Stock on hand, make some according to the directions on page 84, or dissolve 1½ large low-sodium vegetable broth cubes in 5½ cups of hot water.

EACH SERVING PROVIDES:
265calories, 5g protein, 4g fat, 2g dietary fiber
50g carbohydrate, 326mg sodium, 0mg cholesterol

Baked Millet and Sweet Potato Patties with Spinach and Cilantro Sauce

If you have leftover millet on hand, this hearty recipe is a wonderful way to use it. The piquant sauce is a perfect complement to the patties, in both color and flavor. Bright yellow calendula or nasturtium petals make the perfect garnish, if available.

YIELD: 4 MAIN-DISH SERVINGS

The millet
1 cup uncooked millet
2 cups Homemade Vegetable Stock (see NOTE)
¼ teaspoon salt

The patties
1 large sweet potato (about 1 pound)
¼ cup minced fresh parsley leaves
2 tablespoons whole wheat pastry flour
2 tablespoons fresh-squeezed lime juice
1 tablespoon dried oregano, crumbled
2 cloves garlic, minced
2 teaspoons pure chili powder
½ teaspoon salt
2 teaspoons olive oil

The sauce
¼ cup slivered almonds
¾ pound fresh spinach
1 cup chopped fresh cilantro
2 tablespoons fresh-squeezed lime juice
¼ teaspoon salt
Several grinds black pepper

TOAST the millet in a heavy-bottomed pan over high heat, stirring constantly, for about 4 minutes, or until the millet starts to pop. Immediately transfer the millet to a deep bowl and fill the bowl with cold water. Scrub the grains lightly between your palms for a few seconds, then pour into a fine-mesh strainer and rinse under running water for about 1 minute. Set aside to drain.

Bring the stock to a boil in a medium-size saucepan. Add the millet and ¼ teaspoon of the salt, and bring back to a simmer. Lower the heat, cover, and simmer for 20 minutes. Turn off the heat and let stand, covered, for 5 minutes. Transfer to a bowl to cool, fluffing with a fork.

Peel the sweet potato and dice it. Place the pieces on a steamer rack in a saucepan that has a tight-fitting lid. Add about 2 inches of water, cover the pan, and steam over medium-high heat about 20 minutes, until the sweet potato is very soft.

Preheat the oven to 375 degrees F. Place the sweet potato in a food processor, along with the cooled millet, parsley, flour, lime juice, oregano, garlic, chili powder, and ½ teaspoon salt. Process to a thick, homogenous consistency. Lightly oil a baking sheet and your hands. Form the millet mixture into twelve patties and place them on the baking sheet. Bake for 10 minutes, turn the patties over, and bake for an additional 10 minutes.

(continued)

(Baked Millet and Sweet Potato Patties with Spinach
and Cilantro Sauce, *continued*)

While the patties are baking, make the sauce. Place the almonds on a baking sheet and toast in the oven for 8–10 minutes, stirring or shaking the pan occasionally (alternatively, you can toast the almonds in a heavy-bottomed skillet on the stovetop). When the almonds are nicely browned, remove them from the baking sheet and let cool.

Meanwhile, carefully wash the spinach, discarding any thick stems. Place the wet leaves in a stockpot and cover tightly. Turn the heat to medium-high and cook the spinach until wilted, but still bright green, about 3 minutes. Drain briefly in a colander set over a large bowl, then transfer the spinach to a blender. Add the almonds, cilantro, lime juice, salt, pepper, and ½ cup of the reserved spinach cooking liquid. Pulse a few times to chop and combine the ingredients, then puree until smooth.

If necessary, reheat the patties in a warm oven for about 5 minutes. Place 3 of the baked patties on each of 6 warmed serving plates. Top the patties with a portion of the sauce and garnish with nasturtium or calendula petals, if available.

NOTE: If you do not have Homemade Vegetable Stock on hand, make some according to the directions on page 84, or dissolve 1 large low-sodium vegetable broth cube in 2 cups of hot water.

EACH SERVING PROVIDES:
411 calories, 14g protein, 9g fat, 9g dietary fiber
74g carbohydrate, 647mg sodium, 0mg cholesterol

Quinoa, Rice and French Lentil Timbales with Roasted Red Pepper Sauce

Here is a main course with beauty, novelty, and scrumptious flavor. As elegant entrées go, this one is simple to prepare. Use a 1-cup ramekin or bowl to mold the timbales. This dish doesn't need to be piping hot to be delicious; just barely warm is fine. Edible flowers from the garden make the perfect finishing touch on the plates.

YIELD: 4 MAIN-DISH SERVINGS

The timbales
¾ cup uncooked quinoa
3½ cups Homemade Vegetable Stock (see NOTE)
½ cup uncooked tiny French or regular brown lentils
¾ cup uncooked white basmati rice
½ cup minced fresh parsley leaves
2 teaspoons dried oregano
½ teaspoon salt
Several grinds black pepper
4 parsley sprigs

The sauce
2 large red bell peppers
2 tablespoons extra-virgin olive oil
2 tablespoons drained capers
1 clove garlic, minced
¼ teaspoon dried red chile flakes
¼ teaspoon salt

PLACE the quinoa in a large bowl and fill the bowl with water. Wash the quinoa by rubbing it between the palms of your hands for about one minute. Pour the quinoa into a fine-mesh strainer and rinse thoroughly with fresh water. Set aside to drain.

Bring the stock to a boil in a saucepan and add the lentils. Allow to simmer over medium heat, uncovered, for 10 minutes, then add the quinoa, rice, parsley, oregano, salt and pepper and return to a simmer. Cover the pan tightly, reduce the heat to very low, and cook for 20 minutes. Turn off the heat and don't disturb the lid for at least 5 minutes, or until you're ready to make the timbales.

Meanwhile, make the sauce. Preheat the broiler or a gas grill (alternatively, you may use a gas burner on the stovetop). Place the whole bell peppers under the broiler or on the grill and cook for several minutes, until the skin is charred black on one side. Turn the peppers and cook several more minutes to blacken the other side. Continue to turn and cook until the entire skin of the bell peppers is almost uniformly black. Transfer them to a paper or plastic bag, close the bag tightly, and set aside for 10 minutes or so. The steam inside the bag will finish cooking the bell peppers.

When the bell peppers are cool enough to handle, peel them and discard the stems, seeds, and white membranes. Place the peppers in a blender or food processor; add the oil, capers, garlic, chile flakes, and salt. Puree and set aside.

(continued)

(Quinoa, Rice and French Lentil Timbales with Roasted
Red Pepper Sauce, *continued*)

Just before serving, remove the lid of the quinoa mixture and
stir it gently until well combined. Pack the mixture tightly into a
1-cup ramekin or bowl, then turn the ramekin upside down onto
an individual serving plate.Quickly twist and lift the ramekin,
releasing the timbale onto the plate. Surround the timbale with a
"moat" of red pepper sauce, and drizzle some sauce over the top.
Repeat the process for the remaining 3 timbales. Garnish each
timbale with a parsley sprig and serve immediately.

NOTE: If you do not have Homemade Vegetable Stock on
hand, make some according to the directions on page 84, or dissolve 1½ large low-sodium vegetable broth cubes in 3½ cups of
hot water.

EACH SERVING PROVIDES:

440 calories, 16g protein, 10g fat, 12g dietary fiber
75g carbohydrate, 717mg sodium, 0mg cholesterol

SAUTÉS AND STIR-FRIES

* * * * * * * * *

* * * * * * * * *

SAUTÉS AND STIR-FRIES

Tofu with Mushrooms and Miso

Stir-Fry of Cauliflower, Tomatoes, Orange,
    and Fresh Basil

Black Beans Stir-Fried with Broccoli, Corn, and Cilantro

Gingered Spinach and Shiitake Mushrooms

Green Bean, Asparagus, and Tofu Stir-fry over Couscous

Ginger Lemon Stir-Fry

Tempeh with Curry Peanut Sauce

Curried Lentil Stir-Fry with Fennel and Apricots

Lima Beans and Mushrooms in Serrano Chile
    Tomato Sauce

THE SIZZLE OF HOT WOK VEGETABLES and the seductive aroma of sautéed onions are only two of the sensual pleasures offered by stir-fry cooking. We use the term "stir-fry" rather loosely, to encompass pan sautés in addition to wok preparations. Accordingly, we take our flavor inspiration from many of the world's classic cuisines, not only from the Chinese.

Though it requires constant attention at the stove, stir-fry cooking is fast and easy, a terrific way to get a nutritious, made-from-scratch meal on the table when time is short. You can even manage without a recipe—simply sauté fresh vegetables and cooked beans with your favorite seasonings in a hot skillet or wok, and steam Five-Minute Couscous (see page 116) as an accompaniment.

In this chapter, we include some of the convenient main dishes we call upon most frequently.

Tofu with Mushrooms and Miso

ALMOST INSTANT

This simple sauté, quickly concocted from favorite ingredients, will appear on your table frequently.

YIELD: 4 MAIN-DISH SERVINGS

1 cup uncooked white basmati rice
12 ounces firm tofu
1 tablespoon canola oil
1 clove garlic, minced
1 small yellow onion, chopped
1 medium green bell pepper, chopped
6 large button mushrooms, sliced
1 tablespoon dried basil
Scant pinch salt
2 tablespoons light-colored miso
2 tablespoons minced fresh parsley leaves
1 tablespoon apple cider vinegar

BRING 2 cups of water to a boil. Add the rice, return to a boil, cover, and reduce heat to very low. Steam for about 15–20 minutes, until water is absorbed and rice is tender. Allow to stand, covered, for at least 5 minutes before serving.

Meanwhile, dice the tofu into ½-inch cubes and wrap in a tea towel to remove excess moisture. Heat the oil in a wok or heavy skillet over medium heat and sauté the garlic, onion, bell pepper, mushrooms, basil, and salt for 5 minutes, stirring frequently. Add the tofu and sauté 5 minutes longer.

Whisk the miso into ¼ cup water until smooth. Add to the skillet, along with the parsley and vinegar. Remove the pan from the heat and stir until everything is well combined. Fluff the rice and divide it among warmed serving plates. Top with the tofu and serve.

EACH SERVING PROVIDES:

310 calories, 12g protein, 9g fat, 3g dietary fiber
47g carbohydrate, 319mg sodium, 0mg cholesterol

VERSATILE SOY FOODS

The culinary potential of the soy bean was unlocked thousands of years ago in the Far East. Tofu, tempeh, and miso are still important ingredients in the cuisines of Japan, China, Southeast Asia, and Indonesia. These nutritious foods are available at all natural food markets and Asian grocery stores. The blandness of tofu, the "meaty" texture of tempeh, and the salty smoothness of miso lend each to quite distinct but abundant uses.

Stir-Fry of Cauliflower, Tomatoes, Orange, and Fresh Basil

ALMOST INSTANT

This fresh, light dish highlights a vegetable from the crucifer-ous family that is often overlooked as the center of a meal. The rich, smoky flavor of the sesame oil and the peppery character of the fresh basil complement the sweetness of the orange juice perfectly.

YIELD: 4 MAIN-DISH SERVINGS

1 cup uncooked white basmati rice
1 teaspoon olive oil
½ teaspoon granulated garlic
1 tablespoon canola oil
1 tablespoon dark sesame oil
1 medium yellow onion, diced
4 cups chopped cauliflower (about 1 medium head)
½ cup fresh-squeezed orange juice
½ pound fresh pear tomatoes, diced (about 3 medium)
1 can (13 ounces) water-packed tomatillos, drained
   and chopped
½ cup minced fresh basil leaves
1 tablespoon arrowroot powder or cornstarch

BRING 2 cups of water to a boil. Add the rice, olive oil, and gar-lic. Return to a boil, cover, reduce heat to very low, and cook 15–20 minutes, until water is absorbed and rice is tender. Allow to stand, covered, for at least 5 minutes, then fluff with a fork before serving.

   Meanwhile, heat the canola and sesame oils in a wok or heavy skillet over medium-high heat and add the onion. Sauté 2–3 min-utes, until it becomes opaque. Add the cauliflower and stir. Stir in the orange juice, cover, and cook 5 minutes, stirring occasionally. Add the tomatoes, tomatillos, and basil. Stir to combine, lower the heat to medium-low, cover, and cook 5–7 minutes, stirring occasionally, until cauliflower is fork-tender. Combine 2 tablespoons of water with the arrowroot powder in a jar with a tight-fitting lid. Shake to dissolve, then stir into the cauliflower mixture, cooking for a moment or two to thicken the sauce. Place equal portions of the cooked rice on warmed serving plates and spoon the cauliflower mixture over the top.

EACH SERVING PROVIDES:

312 calories, 9g protein, 9g fat, 4g dietary fiber

55g carbohydrate, 43mg sodium, 0mg cholesterol

THE HERB GARDEN

A few fresh herbs growing outside the back door provide a wealth of inspiration for the creative cook. Most herbs are hardy and tolerant of poor growing conditions, so an herb garden is a low-maintenance project. Purchase vigorous seedlings from a reputable nursery and plant them wherever you have a spot of bare soil in the sun. Water as needed and these fragrant plants will provide abundant, convenient, and economical fresh herbs to enliven your cooking throughout the year.

Black Beans Stir-Fried with Broccoli, Corn, and Cilantro

Fresh corn, black beans, and chiles come together to create an irresistible meal. The splash of tequila finishes the dish nicely. If you are using fresh corn, purchase 3 large ears to yield 1½ cups of kernels.

YIELD: 6 MAIN-DISH SERVINGS

1 cup uncooked short-grain brown rice
2 tablespoons canola oil
1 medium white onion, chopped
2 cloves garlic, minced
1 teaspoon cumin seeds, crushed
1 medium red bell pepper, chopped
2 cups chopped broccoli
½ cup fresh-squeezed orange juice
1½ cups fresh or frozen corn kernels
1 can (4 ounces) diced green chiles, drained
1 can (3.8 ounces) olive wedges, drained
1 cup loosely packed minced fresh cilantro leaves
2 cups freshly cooked or canned black beans, drained
2 tablespoons gold tequila

BRING 2 cups of water to a boil. Add the rice, return to a boil, cover, and reduce heat to very low. Steam for about 45–50 minutes, until water is absorbed and rice is tender. Turn off the heat and let stand, covered, at least 5 minutes.

Meanwhile heat the oil over medium heat in a wok or a heavy-bottomed skillet. Add the onion, garlic, and cumin seeds. Sauté for 5 minutes. Stir in the bell pepper, broccoli, and orange juice, and cook 5 minutes. Add the corn, chiles, olives, and cilantro to the skillet.

Sauté 5 more minutes, stirring occasionally. Stir in the black beans and tequila, toss to combine, and heat through. Place equal portions of the cooked rice on warmed serving plates and spoon the black bean mixture over the top. Serve immediately.

EACH SERVING PROVIDES:

338 calories, 12g protein, 8g fat, 8g dietary fiber

56g carbohydrate, 345mg sodium, 0mg cholesterol

Gingered Spinach and Shiitake Mushrooms

This classic Chinese spinach preparation is simple and quick to prepare. The shiitake mushrooms and ginger complement the tender, fresh spinach, and the rice soaks up all of the delicious sauce.

YIELD: 4 MAIN-DISH SERVINGS

1 ounce dried shiitake mushrooms
1 cup uncooked long-grain white rice (not "converted")
1½ pounds fresh spinach (about 2 bunches)
2 teaspoons peanut oil
½ medium yellow onion, chopped
1 tablespoon grated fresh ginger
2 teaspoons low-sodium soy sauce
2 teaspoons arrowroot powder or cornstarch

SOAK the mushrooms in 2 cups of hot water for 30 minutes. Lift the mushrooms from their soaking liquid, reserving the liquid. Rinse the mushrooms under a thin stream of cold, running water, rubbing to remove any grit lodged in the membranes under the caps. Squeeze the mushrooms gently to remove some of the liquid. Discard the mushroom stems and sliver the caps. Set aside. Strain the soaking liquid through a paper coffee filter. Set aside ⅓ cup of the soaking liquid for the spinach. Add water to the remaining soaking liquid to measure 2 cups for the rice. Bring the 2 cups of liquid to a boil and add the rice. Return to a boil, cover, reduce the heat to very low, and cook for 15–20 minutes, until liquid is absorbed and rice is tender. Let stand, covered, at least 5 minutes, then fluff with a fork before serving.

Meanwhile, wash the spinach and discard the stems. Set the wet leaves aside. In a heavy-bottomed skillet or wok that has a tight-fitting lid, heat the oil over medium heat, then stir in the onion and ginger. Sauté for 2–3 minutes, stirring almost constantly, until the onion begins to wilt. Pile in the spinach leaves and immediately cover the pan. Cook for about 4–6 minutes, until the spinach wilts.

In a jar that has a tight-fitting lid, shake the soy sauce and arrowroot powder together with the reserved ⅓ cup of mushroom soaking liquid. Add the arrowroot mixture and slivered mushrooms to the skillet and cook, stirring constantly, about 2 minutes, until a thick sauce develops. Spoon the rice onto warm serving plates and top with the spinach. Serve immediately, with sesame seeds and soy sauce, if desired.

EACH SERVING PROVIDES:

259 calories, 8g protein, 3g fat, 4g dietary fiber
52g carbohydrate, 207mg sodium, 0mg cholesterol

Green Bean, Asparagus, and Tofu Stir-Fry over Couscous

ALMOST INSTANT

This recipe takes advantage of two of spring's most delicious vegetables—asparagus and green beans. The flavors, colors, and textures harmonize to produce a delicious meal.

YIELD: 4 MAIN-DISH SERVINGS

¾ pound asparagus
½ pound green beans
½ pound firm tofu
1 tablespoon dark sesame oil
3 tablespoons rice wine vinegar
½ white onion, diced
1 clove garlic, minced
1 medium red bell pepper, chopped
1½ cups uncooked couscous
½ teaspoon granulated garlic
Several grinds black pepper
¼ cup minced fresh parsley leaves
1 tablespoon grated fresh ginger

BREAK off and discard the tough stem ends of the asparagus. Cut the asparagus at a slant into 1-inch pieces. Snap off the ends of the beans and pull off any strings. Cut the beans at a slant into 1-inch pieces. Drain the tofu and pat it dry with a tea towel or paper towel. Cut into ½-inch cubes.

Heat the sesame oil and rice wine vinegar in a wok and heat over medium-high heat. Stir in the onion and garlic and cook for about 3 minutes. Add the asparagus, green beans, and bell

pepper and stir to combine. Cover and cook, stirring occasionally, for 8–10 minutes, until the asparagus and beans are barely fork-
tender. Stir in the tofu, parsley, and ginger. Cook, uncovered, for
3–4 minutes.

Meanwhile, bring 2¼ cups of water to a boil. Add the couscous, granulated garlic, and black pepper and stir to combine.
Cover and immediately remove from the heat. Let sit undisturbed
for 5 minutes.

Fluff the couscous with a fork then evenly distribute on 4 serving plates. Top with the asparagus mixture. Serve with soy sauce,
if desired.

EACH SERVING PROVIDES:

404 calories, 16g protein, 8g fat, 6g dietary fiber

68g carbohydrate, 20mg sodium, 0mg cholesterol

Ginger Lemon Stir-Fry

ALMOST INSTANT

The vegetables and tempeh are delicately cooked and infused with a wonderful ginger flavor. Serve with fragrant, hot jasmine tea.

YIELD: 4 MAIN-DISH SERVINGS

1½ cups uncooked brown basmati rice
Pinch salt
2 tablespoons arrowroot powder or cornstarch
¼ cup fresh-squeezed lemon juice
3 tablespoons brown rice syrup
1 tablespoon grated fresh ginger
1 tablespoon low-sodium soy sauce
2 tablespoons light-colored miso
2 tablespoons canola oil
1 medium yellow onion, diced
2½ cups chopped broccoli
4 ounces tempeh, cubed
½ pound mushrooms, sliced (2 cups)
½ pound snow peas, strings removed
1 can (8 ounces) water chestnuts, drained and sliced
2 tablespoons mirin

BRING 3 cups of water to a boil, add the rice and salt. Return to a boil and cover the pot. Reduce heat to very low and simmer 25–30 minutes, until the water is absorbed and the rice is tender. Allow the rice to stand in the covered pot for at least 5 minutes, then fluff with a fork before serving.

Meanwhile, combine the arrowroot powder with ¾ cup of cold water in a small bowl. Whisk in the lemon juice, rice syrup, ginger, and soy sauce. Set aside. In a separate small bowl, blend the miso with 2 tablespoons water until smooth, and set aside.

Heat the oil over medium heat in a wok or heavy-bottomed skillet, then add the onion. Stir and cook about 2 minutes, then add the broccoli and tempeh. Cook 5 minutes, stirring frequently. Stir in the mushrooms, snow peas, water chestnuts, mirin, and ¼ cup hot water. Stir-fry about 4 more minutes. Stir the arrowroot mixture to recombine it, then add it to the skillet and increase the heat to medium-high. Cook about 2 minutes, stirring frequently, until the sauce thickens. Quickly stir in the miso and immediately transfer to a warmed serving bowl. Serve hot with hot rice.

EACH SERVING PROVIDES:
652 calories, 16g protein, 12g fat, 9g dietary fiber
122g carbohydrate, 511mg sodium, 0mg cholesterol

Tempeh with Curry Peanut Sauce

This unusual combination of ingredients creates a deliciously rich dish. After your first taste, it is hard to get enough.

YIELD: 4 MAIN-DISH SERVINGS

1 cup uncooked bulgur wheat

The sauce
1½ tablespoons creamy peanut butter
2 tablespoons fresh-squeezed lemon juice
1½ tablespoons brown rice syrup
1 tablespoon light-colored miso
½ cup hot water
1 teaspoon low-sodium soy sauce

The stir-fry
1 large carrot
2 ribs celery
2 tablespoons canola oil
2 cloves garlic, minced
1 medium red onion, chopped
8 ounces tempeh, cubed
1 tablespoon curry powder
1 tablespoon dried oregano
1 teaspoon chili powder
4 fresh lemon wedges

BRING 2 cups of water to a boil. Stir in the bulgur, cover, reduce heat to low, and steam 15 minutes. Let stand an additional 5 minutes, then fluff with a fork before serving.

Meanwhile, whisk together the sauce ingredients and set aside. Cut the carrot and celery into 1-inch matchsticks and set aside. Heat the oil over medium heat in a wok or heavy-bottomed skillet and add the garlic, onion, carrot, celery, tempeh, curry powder, oregano, and chili powder. Stir-fry 2 minutes. Pour in the peanut sauce and increase the heat a little to bring it to a simmer. Cover and continue to cook, stirring frequently, for about 7 minutes, until the vegetables are tender-crisp. Divide the bulgur among warmed serving plates and top with the stir-fry. Serve immediately, with lemon wedges.

EACH SERVING PROVIDES:

395 calories, 18g protein, 16g fat, 9g dietary fiber

51g carbohydrate, 277mg sodium, 0mg cholesterol

Curried Lentil Stir-Fry with Fennel and Apricots

This delicious lentil dish has several easy steps. Get out your spices and dice the vegetables while the lentils and rice are cooking. Add a lemony salad and sesame crackers to round out the feast.

YIELD: 6 MAIN-DISH SERVINGS

1 cup dried brown lentils
1½ cups uncooked white basmati rice
16 dried apricot halves (about 4 ounces)
2 tablespoons canola oil
1 medium yellow onion, diced
3 cloves garlic, minced
1 teaspoon ground cumin
1 teaspoon ground turmeric
½ teaspoon ground coriander
½ teaspoon ground cinnamon
⅛ teaspoon cayenne
2 cups chopped broccoli
1 cup diced carrot
1 cup diced fresh fennel bulb (about 1 medium)

SORT and rinse the lentils, discarding any small pebbles you may find. Bring 4 cups of water to a boil over high heat, then add the lentils. Return to a boil, reduce the heat to medium-low, and simmer gently, covered, for 25–30 minutes, until the lentils are just tender. Do not overcook or they will be mushy.

Meanwhile, in a separate saucepan, bring 3 cups of water to a boil. Add the rice, return to a boil, cover, and reduce heat to low. Cook 15–20 minutes, until the water is absorbed and the rice is tender. Allow to stand, covered, at least 5 minutes, then fluff with a fork before serving. Thinly slice the apricot halves and place them in a bowl. Pour ½ cup of hot water over them, cover, and set aside.

Heat the oil in a wok or heavy-bottomed skillet over medium heat. Add the onion, garlic, cumin, turmeric, coriander, cinnamon, and cayenne. Sauté for several minutes, tossing to coat the onion with the spices. Drain the apricots, reserving their soaking liquid. Add the liquid to the wok. Stir in the broccoli, carrot, and fennel. Cover the wok and steam the vegetables for 7–10 minutes, until they are fork-tender. Add the apricots and lentils and toss to combine. Serve over the rice.

EACH SERVING PROVIDES:

425 calories, 16g protein, 6g fat, 9g dietary fiber
81g carbohydrate, 42mg sodium, 0mg cholesterol

Lima Beans and Mushrooms in Serrano Chile Tomato Sauce

This recipe uses fresh shiitake mushrooms in a delicious and unconventional way. Select fairly large ones of similar size, if possible. If you have cooked beans on hand, this dish comes together quickly and easily and is a great choice for an impromptu dinner party on a chilly evening. Add couscous steamed in a hearty vegetable stock and a leafy, tart salad for a wonderful winter feast.

YIELD: 4 MAIN-DISH SERVINGS

2 fresh serrano chiles
1 can (28 ounces) whole pear tomatoes, undrained
3 cloves garlic
½ cup firmly packed fresh cilantro leaves
2 tablespoons fresh-squeezed lime juice
⅛ teaspoon plus ¼ teaspoon salt
¼ pound fresh shiitake mushrooms
½ pound button mushrooms
2 tablespoons olive oil
2 cups freshly cooked or canned lima beans, drained
1 cup fresh or frozen shelled green peas (about 1 pound of English pea pods)
¼ cup Madeira or dry sherry
Several grinds black pepper

REMOVE and discard the stems of the chiles. (Also remove the seeds for a less spicy dish.) In a blender or food processor, combine the chiles, undrained tomatoes, garlic, cilantro, lime juice, and the ⅛ teaspoon salt. Puree to a smooth consistency and set aside. Gently wipe the mushrooms clean with a damp tea towel. Cut the shiitakes into ¼-inch slices. Quarter the button mushrooms.

Heat the oil over medium heat in a heavy-bottomed skillet or Dutch oven. Add all the mushrooms and sauté for 3–4 minutes, until they begin to turn golden. Add the tomato mixture—careful, it may splatter—and the lima beans. Cook over medium-low heat, stirring frequently, about 15 minutes, until the sauce has reduced to a nice, thick consistency. If you are using fresh shelled peas, add them for the last 5–6 minutes of cooking time. If you are using frozen peas, rinse briefly to melt the ice crystals, drain, and add them for the last 2 minutes of the cooking time. Stir in the Madeira and plenty of pepper and heat through for another minute. Serve very hot.

EACH SERVING PROVIDES:

292 calories, 14g protein, 8g fat, 12g dietary fiber
42g carbohydrate, 532mg sodium, 0mg cholesterol

A WARMING WINTER REPAST

• •

Fresh sliced jicama with lime juice

Lima Beans and Mushrooms in Serrano Chile
Tomato Sauce, page 190

Five-Minute Couscous, page 116

Shredded cabbage with lemon-oregano dressing

Walnuts and port

ENTRÉES FROM
THE OVEN

* * * * * * * *

* * * * * * * *

ENTRÉES FROM THE OVEN

Stuffed Artichokes with Lemon Dill Dipping Sauce

Porcini Mushroom Nut Loaf with Dijon Cream Sauce

Baked Onions Stuffed with Minted Couscous

Roasted Vegetable Supper with Garlic, Rosemary,
and Tart Greens

Oven-Braised Tempeh and New Potatoes with
Mustard and Sauerkraut

Potatoes, Zucchini, and Mushrooms Baked in Broth

Eggplant Casserole with Tofu, Olives, and
Herbed Tomato Sauce

Tomatoes and Couscous en Papillote with
Sherry and Cilantro

Pizza with Fresh Basil, Capers, and Pine Nuts

Pizza with Salsa Verde, Tomatoes, and Olives

Grilled Eggplant and Pepper Pizza with Baked Garlic

Pizza with Black Beans, Avocado, and Cilantro

Basic Pizza Crust

WINTER GATHERINGS, especially around the holidays, traditionally feature a hearty, long-baked main course. On such occasions, the kitchen becomes the warm and cozy heart of our homes. In warm weather, the grill can become an outdoor oven, turning the backyard into a summer kitchen for memorable al fresco entertaining.

Any of the recipes in this chapter can provide an imaginative centerpiece for just such a vegan feast. Many can be prepared in advance or, in the case of pizza or papillote dishes, put together quickly for an impromptu dinner party. Simply add an appetizer or two that complement the theme, perhaps a vegetable side dish, and a refreshing, leafy salad to finish the meal.

From simple to elaborate in their preparation, the following baked entrées are hearty, satisfying fare. Steaming hot from the oven or grill, they arrive at the table fragrant, sizzling, and infinitely inviting.

Stuffed Artichokes with Lemon Dill Dipping Sauce

These stuffed artichokes are a little labor intensive but not difficult to prepare. The result is well worth the effort, since your guests will be delighted with this special treat. Include whole grain bread and a hearty salad, if you wish.

YIELD: 6 MAIN-DISH SERVINGS

The sauce
1 cup tofu mayonnaise
1 tablespoon minced fresh dill leaves
1 teaspoon fresh-squeezed lemon juice
½ teaspoon lemon extract
A few grinds black pepper

The artichokes
6 large artichokes
2 bay leaves
1 teaspoon granulated garlic

The stuffing
½ ounce dried shiitake mushrooms
1 tablespoon olive oil
3 cloves garlic, minced
1 small yellow onion, minced
1 small red bell pepper, minced
2 tablespoons fresh-squeezed lemon juice
2 cups coarse dry bread crumbs
2 tablespoons minced fresh dill leaves
⅛ teaspoon salt
Several grinds black pepper
¼ cup dry white wine

WHISK together the sauce ingredients and set aside in the refrigerator so flavors can blend. Bring a few quarts of water to a boil in a large stockpot. Rinse the artichokes, cut their stems to within ½ inch of the base, and cut crosswise to remove 1 inch of the tips of the artichokes. Remove any damaged or stubby outer leaves. Add the bay leaves and garlic to the stockpot, then drop in the artichokes and put a lid on the pot, leaving it ajar so steam can escape. Boil for about 25 minutes, until tender enough at the base to pierce easily with a knife. Do not overcook the artichokes; they will cook a little more in the oven. Remove from the pot, rinse in cold water, and set aside until thoroughly cooled.

Meanwhile, cover the mushrooms with 2 cups of hot water in a shallow bowl. Soak for 30 minutes. Lift the mushrooms from the soaking liquid and strain the liquid through cheesecloth or a paper coffee filter. Reserve the liquid. Carefully wash the mushrooms under a thin stream of running water to remove any grit that may be lodged in the layers of membrane under the caps. Remove the tough stems, and finely chop the mushrooms. Set aside.

Preheat the oven to 350 degrees F. Heat the olive oil in a skillet over medium heat. Sauté the garlic, onion, bell pepper, and mushrooms for about 7 minutes, until limp. Stir the lemon juice into the skillet, then combine the sautéed vegetables with the bread crumbs, dill, salt, and pepper in a mixing bowl until everything is well distributed. Stir the wine into 1½ cups of the reserved mushroom soaking liquid. Add to the stuffing and stir until you have a well-moistened mixture.

(continued)

(Stuffed Artichokes with Lemon Dill Dipping Sauce, *continued*)

Cut the cooked artichokes in half lengthwise. Use a spoon to scrape out the fuzzy inner "choke" and fill each half with stuffing. You can mound up the filling; it will stay put during baking. Pour about ¾ cup water in the bottom of a high-walled baking pan. Place the artichokes, stuffing side up, in the pan. Cover with aluminum foil and bake for 20 minutes. Remove the foil and continue to bake for 10 minutes. Serve hot, with the sauce on the side.

EACH SERVING PROVIDES:

329 calories, 9g protein, 12g fat, 8g dietary fiber

46g carbohydrate, 685mg sodium, 0mg cholestrol

SOME FACTS ABOUT FATS

In the past decade, the media has jumped on the nutrition bandwagon and scared us all away from fat. It is true that saturated fat and dietary cholesterol pose health risks for people with a history of heart disease and those with elevated blood lipids. For them, the vegan diet makes great sense since it is extremely low in both substances. But it is important to remember that fats perform very important functions in the body—among other things, they transport nutrients, lubricate cells, and help regulate hormone production. Mono-unsaturated fats (such as olive oil) and omega-3 fats (such as flaxseed oil) provide these "essential" fatty acids and should be included in the diet, especially by vegans. Of course, moderation is a wise approach, because fat is a high-calorie nutrient. Health experts generally agree that we should derive no more than 20 to 30 percent of our daily calories from fat.

Porcini Mushroom Nut Loaf with Dijon Cream Sauce

This loaf—a bit high in fat for a commonplace dinner—makes a standout main course for Thanksgiving or any very special occasion. It can be prepared in advance and allowed to sit at room temperature for several hours, then baked as described. Serve it with baked sweet potatoes, steamed green beans, crusty bread, and a salad for a sumptuous feast.

YIELD: 8 MAIN-DISH SERVINGS

The loaf
1 ounce dried porcini mushrooms
1 cup uncooked long-grain brown rice
½ pound button mushrooms
1 tablespoon olive oil
4 tablespoons dry sherry
1 medium yellow onion, chopped
3 cloves garlic, minced
1 teaspoon dried marjoram
1 teaspoon dried sage
½ teaspoon dried thyme
1 cup raw walnuts
½ cup raw cashews
½ cup raw sunflower seeds
2 tablespoons arrowroot powder

The sauce
1½ cups plain soy milk
2 tablespoons unbleached flour
1 tablespoon arrowroot powder
2 tablespoons Dijon mustard
1 tablespoon olive oil

Pour 3 cups of hot water over the porcini mushrooms in a saucepan. Cover the pan and steep for 30 minutes. Lift the mushrooms out, reserving the soaking liquid. Chop the mushrooms and set aside. Strain the soaking liquid through a paper coffee filter and place 2½ cups of it back in the saucepan and bring to a boil. Reserve the remaining soaking liquid for use in the loaf. Add the brown rice to the boiling liquid, cover, and simmer over low heat for 40–50 minutes, until all the liquid is absorbed and the rice is tender. Remove from the heat and allow to sit, covered, for about 5 minutes.

Meanwhile, brush or wipe any dirt from the button mushrooms and chop them. Place the oil and 2 tablespoons of the sherry in a skillet over medium heat and add the onion and garlic. Sauté for about 2 minutes, then stir in the button mushrooms, marjoram, sage, and thyme. Sauté for 10 minutes, then add the chopped porcini mushrooms and continue to cook for about 5 minutes, until almost all of the liquid has evaporated.

Preheat the oven to 375 degrees F. Place the walnuts in a single layer in a dry, heavy-bottomed skillet over medium-high heat. Shake the pan frequently. Soon the nuts will be golden brown, emitting a wonderful roasted aroma. Remove immediately from the pan and set aside. Separately toast the cashews and sunflower seeds in the same manner. Finely chop the nuts.

Spoon the cooked rice into a food processor and add the toasted nuts. Pulse to combine, but do not puree. Measure the reserved mushroom soaking liquid and add water, if necessary, to make ¼ cup. Place it in a small jar that has a tight-fitting lid. Add the arrowroot powder, cover tightly, and shake to dissolve. Pour this into the rice mixture along with the remaining 2 tablespoons of sherry and pulse to combine.

Lightly oil a 9 × 5 × 3-inch loaf pan. Cut a piece of parchment paper big enough to line the bottom and sides of the pan, allowing a few inches of overhang. Place the parchment in the pan, pleating it to conform to the corners. Lightly oil the paper. Use your hands to form the mushroom mixture into a roll shape down the center of the pan, extending from one end of the pan to the other and allowing about 1 inch of space between the roll and the sides of the pan on both sides. Evenly pat the rice mixture over the top and around the sides of the mushroom roll. Wrap the overlapping parchment over the top of the loaf, then cover with foil. Place the loaf in the oven and bake for 30 minutes. Remove from the oven and place on a wire rack to cool in the pan for 10 minutes. Remove the foil and fold back the parchment paper, then invert the loaf onto a serving platter. Allow it to sit for an additional 5–10 minutes before serving, or it will crumble when sliced.

Meanwhile, prepare the sauce. Place ½ cup of the soy milk in a small jar that has a tight-fitting lid. Add the flour and arrowroot, cover tightly, and shake to dissolve. Place the remaining 1 cup soy milk in a bowl and whisk in the flour mixture. Whisk in the mustard and oil, then transfer to a saucepan. Cook over medium heat, stirring occasionally, until it thickens, about 4–5 minutes. Transfer to a warm serving bowl or gravy boat. Cut the loaf into slices and serve, passing the sauce.

EACH SERVING PROVIDES:
390 calories, 10g protein, 24g fat, 3g dietary fiber
37g carbohydrate, 115mg sodium, 0mg cholestrol

A SIMPLE STANDBY SAUCE

This delicious soy-based cream sauce has a velvety consistency and nearly infinite uses. Here are two ideas: Add snipped fresh tarragon to create a perfect sauce for early Spring peas, or thin it with a little wine or broth and add sautéed fresh vegetables for a delicious topping for pasta.

Entrées from the Oven
••••

Baked Onions Stuffed with Minted Couscous

Walla Walla onions are perfect for this unusual dish: They have a slightly sweet flavor that complements the fresh mint. Select onions that have a uniform shape and are slightly flat on the bottom, if possible. Serve this succulent entrée with fresh crusty bread and a garbanzo bean and green leaf salad.

YIELD: 4 MAIN-DISH SERVINGS

⅓ cup minced dried tomatoes (see NOTE)
4 large yellow onions
¾ cup dried couscous
2 tablespoons olive oil
1 tablespoon red wine vinegar
¼ cup minced fresh mint leaves
¼ teaspoon salt
⅛ teaspoon ground black pepper
2 tablespoons dry sherry

The sauce
3 tablespoons olive oil
1 tablespoon balsamic vinegar
¼ teaspoon salt
Several grinds black pepper

BRING several quarts to a boil in a large stockpot. Peel the onions, leaving them whole, and drop them into the boiling water. Return the pot to a boil and cook for 15 minutes. Drain and set aside to cool. Preheat the oven to 350 degrees F.

Heat 1½ cups water to a boil and stir in the couscous. Cover and immediately turn off the heat. Let stand 5 minutes, then remove the lid and transfer the couscous to a bowl, fluffing with a fork to break up any large clumps. Whisk together the olive oil and vinegar. Stir in the dried tomatoes, mint, salt, and pepper. Combine this mixture with the couscous.

When the onions are cool enough to handle, barely trim the bottoms so they will sit flat. Slice 1 inch from the top of each onion to expose the inside. Scoop out and reserve the onion centers, being careful not to cut into the 3 outer onion layers. If the bottom develops a "hole," patch it from the inside with a piece of the scooped out onion. Use some of the couscous to gently fill each onion and stand the filled onions upright in a baking dish. Reserve the remaining couscous. Add hot water to the baking dish to a depth of about 1 inch, and add the sherry. Bake, uncovered, for 45 minutes.

While the onions are baking, mince the reserved onion to measure ½ cup. Stir it into the remaining couscous and set aside. Whisk together the sauce ingredients and warm over low heat for a few minutes just before serving. When the onions are almost done, briefly reheat the reserved couscous over low heat or in a microwave oven and arrange equal amounts on warm serving plates. Place a cooked onion in the center of each mound of couscous and drizzle with the sauce. Serve immediately.

NOTE: If the dried tomatoes are too dry to mince, soak them in hot water 15–30 minutes. Drain the tomatoes and mince them.

EACH SERVING PROVIDES:
361 calories, 7g protein, 18g fat, 4g dietary fiber
45g carbohydrate, 362mg sodium, 0mg cholestrol

Roasted Vegetable Supper with Garlic, Rosemary, and Tart Greens

This entrée is a wonderfully simple and healthy way to celebrate the corn harvest. Include Five-Minute Couscous (page 108), a salad, and bread to round out the meal.

YIELD: 8 MAIN-DISH SERVINGS

The roast
8 ears fresh corn, with husks
2 pounds tiny red potatoes
3 medium carrots
2 bulbs garlic
1 tablespoon olive oil
6 sprigs (4 inches each) fresh rosemary

The greens
1½ pounds fresh Swiss chard (about 2 bunches)
2 cups finely shredded red cabbage
1 tablespoon olive oil
2 tablespoons fresh-squeezed lemon juice
Pinch salt
A few grinds black pepper

PREHEAT the oven to 400 degrees F. Peel back the husks of the corn, but do not remove them. Remove the silk, then rewrap corn cobs in husks. Twist husks at the top to create as tight a compartment for the corn as possible. If the husks have been trimmed so you cannot twist them closed, wrap the end of the corn with some string to keep the husks in place. Soak the corn in cool water for about 30 minutes, then drain and blot dry, and set aside.

Meanwhile, scrub the potatoes and the carrots. If the potatoes are very small, leave them whole; otherwise, cut them in halves or quarters so that all potato pieces are of uniform size. Cut the carrots in half lengthwise and then into 3-inch lengths. Remove excess papery skin from the bulbs of garlic but don't break them into individual cloves. Rub the vegetables with the olive oil. Arrange them in a single layer in a large baking dish or roasting pan. Arrange the rosemary sprigs among the vegetables and bake for 1 hour, until vegetables are tender. Add the corn to the roasting pan 30 minutes into the cooking time.

Meanwhile, carefully wash the chard and thinly slice the stem portion. Do not dry the chard leaves; tear them into large pieces and mound them in a large stockpot along with the sliced stems and the shredded cabbage. A few minutes before the roasted vegetables are ready, put a lid on the stockpot and steam over medium heat for 10 minutes (there is no need to add water, as the water that clings to the chard will be sufficient). When wilted, drain. Toss with the olive oil, lemon juice, salt, and pepper.

Arrange the steamed chard and cabbage in a mound in the center of a large platter and place the roasted vegetables around them, placing a bulb of garlic on each end of the platter. People can help themselves to the various vegetables and to individual cloves of garlic which, when squeezed, will produce a deliciously mild garlic paste to spread on the corn or on bread.

EACH SERVING PROVIDES:
251 calories, 7g protein, 5g fat, 9g dietary fiber
51g carbohydrate, 205mg sodium, 0mg cholestrol

Oven-Braised Tempeh and New Potatoes with Mustard and Sauerkraut

This meatless sauerkraut bake is a wonderful treat for fans of the pickled cabbage. It is simple to prepare and makes a hearty main course for a wintry evening. If you can't find bite-size potatoes, cut larger potatoes into chunks no larger than about 2 inches square. A delicious one-pot meal when served with a thick-crusted country rye bread.

YIELD: 4 MAIN-DISH SERVINGS

8 ounces tempeh
2 tablespoons olive oil
1 medium yellow onion, diced
2 carrots, cut into ¼-inch slices
1 pound bite-size new potatoes
2 cups low-sodium sauerkraut
2 tablespoons Dijon mustard
2 teaspoons Hungarian paprika
1 teaspoon caraway seed
½ teaspoon salt
Several grinds black pepper

PREHEAT the oven to 350 degrees F. Cut the tempeh into 4 pieces of equal size. Heat the oil over medium heat in a large oven-proof skillet that has a tight-fitting lid. Lightly brown the tempeh on both sides, then transfer the tempeh to a plate and sauté the onion in the same pan for 2 minutes. Return the tempeh to the pan, top with the carrots and potatoes, and turn off the heat. Add the sauerkraut in an even layer on top of the vegetables.

Stir together the mustard, paprika, caraway seed, salt, and pepper in a bowl, then add 1½ cups of water and stir to combine. Pour this mixture into the pan and cover the pan tightly. Bake for 45 minutes, until the vegetables are fork tender. Serve very hot in warmed shallow bowls.

EACH SERVING PROVIDES:

336 calories, 15g protein, 12g fat, 11g dietary fiber
46g carbohydrate, 1271mg sodium, 0mg cholesterol

TOFU'S LESSER-KNOWN COUSIN

Tempeh is more proof of the humble soybean's versatility. The soybeans are fermented, producing a high-protein, high-fiber, high-enzyme slab found in the refrigerator case at natural-food markets. The flavor of tempeh is nutty and its texture is chewy, in contrast to tofu's bland and soft nature.

Potatoes, Zucchini, and Mushrooms Baked in Broth

This all-vegetable dish is wonderful. Bake it on a cool autumn day when you want your house to be filled with the aroma of marjoram.

YIELD: 6 MAIN-DISH SERVINGS

½ teaspoon canola oil
1 pound russet potatoes (about 2 medium)
⅔ pound zucchini (about 2 medium)
1 medium red bell pepper
1 cup Homemade Vegetable Stock (see NOTE)
1 medium yellow onion, diced
2 tablespoons unbleached flour
2 teaspoons dried marjoram
1 can (4¼ ounces) chopped black olives
½ pound button mushrooms, sliced (2 cups)
¼ cup fine dry bread crumbs

PREHEAT the oven to 350 degrees F. Rub a 10 × 10 × 2-inch baking dish with the oil and set it aside. Scrub the potatoes and thinly slice them. Wash the zucchini, trim off the ends, and thinly slice lengthwise. Remove the stem and seeds from the red bell pepper, wash it, then thinly slice it lengthwise. Heat the stock briefly, but do not boil.

Layer a third of the potatoes on the bottom of the baking dish and cover with a third of the onions. Sprinkle ½ tablespoon of the flour evenly over the onions. Repeat this process. Sprinkle with

1 teaspoon of the marjoram, then layer on all of the bell pepper and all of the olives. Top that with all of the mushroom slices and make a layer with all of the zucchini slices. Dust with the remaining 1 tablespoon of flour. Crumble on the remaining 1 teaspoon of marjoram, then cover with the remaining onions and potato slices. Pour the broth over the vegetables, then sprinkle on the bread crumbs. Cover and bake 45 minutes. Remove the cover and continue to bake for 15 minutes. Remove from the oven and allow to cool for 5 minutes before serving.

NOTE: If you do not have Homemade Vegetable Stock on hand, make some using the directions on page 84, or dissolve ½ large low-sodium vegetable broth cube in 1 cup of hot water.

EACH SERVING PROVIDES:

162 calories, 4g protein, 3g fat, 3g dietary fiber
31g carbohydrate, 205mg sodium, 0mg cholesterol

POTATO VARIETY

Potatoes are versatile, tasty, and enjoyed by adults and children alike. The russet is the most popular potato, followed by the red and white types, but many lesser known varieties are available. Unusual potatoes such as Yellow Finns and Blue Caribs now frequently appear in gourmet produce markets. They provide distinctly different colors, textures, and flavors. Potato lovers will want to seek them out.

Eggplant Casserole with Tofu, Olives, and Herbed Tomato Sauce

The colors of the layered vegetables in this summertime casserole are pleasing and the flavors delightful. Be sure to use a fresh, glossy, unblemished eggplant for best results.

YIELD: 6 MAIN-DISH SERVINGS

¼ teaspoon olive oil
10 ounces firm tofu
1 can (15 ounces) tomato sauce
1 cup canned tomato puree
¼ cup minced calamata olives
¼ cup dry sherry
1½ tablespoons dried oregano, crushed
4 cloves garlic, minced
Several grinds black pepper
3 medium zucchini (about 1 pound)
2 medium fresh tomatoes (about 1 pound)
1 medium eggplant (about 1 pound)
6 slices oatmeal bread or other chewy, whole grain bread
1 medium yellow onion, diced

USE the oil to rub down a 3½-quart casserole dish. Drain the tofu and cut it into ¼-inch slices. Place the slices on a tea towel to drain off the surface water. Preheat the oven to 350 degrees F.

Stir together the tomato sauce, tomato puree, olives, sherry, oregano, garlic, and pepper and set aside. Cut off the ends of the zucchini and cut it lengthwise into ¼-inch slices. Cut out the stem ends of the tomatoes and cut them crosswise into ¼-inch slices. Peel the eggplant, discarding the stem, and cut it crosswise into ¼-inch slices.

Place ¼ cup of the sauce in the bottom of the casserole dish and spread it around. Top with a layer of the eggplant slices, then a layer of the zucchini slices. Distribute half of the onion over the zucchini, then top evenly with all of the tofu slices and all of the bread slices. (Depending on your pan size, you may need fewer slices to make a single layer of bread. It is all right if the slices overlap a bit.) Top the bread evenly with all of the tomato slices, then with half of the remaining sauce. Add the remaining onion, the remaining eggplant, then the remaining zucchini. Spread the remaining sauce evenly over the zucchini and gently shake the dish to settle its contents. Cover, and bake for 45–50 minutes, until the vegetables are fork-tender all the way through the casserole. Remove the lid and allow the casserole to stand at room temperature 5–10 minutes before cutting. Serve hot.

EACH SERVING PROVIDES:

221 calories, 10g protein, 9g fat, 6g dietary fiber
30g carbohydrate, 651mg sodium, 0mg cholesterol

Tomatoes and Couscous en Papillote with Sherry and Cilantro

The vibrant red, green, and yellow of this meal-in-a-packet make a beautiful presentation. And that is just the beginning—the aroma and flavor are also sensational. Once you are familiar with the folding and sealing techniques, parchment paper preparations such as this one come together very quickly. Serve this as a light main dish along with warmed corn tortillas and spicy black beans.

YIELD: 4 MAIN-DISH SERVINGS

2 pounds fresh pear tomatoes
   (or about 9 canned whole pear tomatoes)
¼ cup dry sherry
½ teaspoon granulated garlic
½ teaspoon ground cumin
½ teaspoon chili powder
1 teaspoon olive oil
¾ cup dried couscous
1 cup fresh or frozen shelled peas (about 1 pound English
   pea pods)
¼ cup minced fresh cilantro leaves
4 green onions, sliced into 1-inch lengths

4 pieces (12 × 16 inches each) parchment paper for baking

BLANCH the fresh tomatoes by immersing them in boiling water 1–2 minutes. Immediately plunge them into cold water. When the tomatoes are cool enough to handle, peel them. Cut out and discard the stem ends, and chop them coarsely, retaining their juices. Set the tomatoes aside in a bowl. (Alternatively, briefly drain the canned tomatoes, reserving the juice for another use, such as soup stock. Chop the tomatoes to measure 1⅓ cups and, without draining further, set them aside in a bowl.)

Preheat the oven to 425 degrees F. Combine the sherry, ¼ cup water, garlic, cumin, and chili powder in a small bowl and set aside.

Fold each piece of parchment in half and crease to create 8 × 12-inch rectangles. Use scissors to cut each folded rectangle into a large half-heart shape.

Open out one of the hearts and rub one side of it with ¼ teaspoon of the oil. Place 3 tablespoons of the couscous near the center of the crease on the oiled side of the parchment. Top with ⅓ cup of the chopped tomatoes with juice, then with ¼ cup of the peas. Distribute one-quarter of the cilantro and onions over the top, then pour 2 tablespoons of the sherry mixture over the vegetables and couscous. Close the heart so that the edges of the paper meet. Working carefully to avoid losing any of the liquid, fold over ½ inch of the paper at the round end and press firmly to crease. Work your way around the shape of the heart, folding in the edges and creasing sharply in overlapping pleats. Twist the pointy end tightly to seal everything inside the paper packet. Repeat this process to fill and seal the remaining packets.

Place the packets in a single layer on a baking sheet and bake for 15 minutes. Place each packet on a warmed serving plate and instruct your guests to pinch and tear the paper to release the aromatic steam. The contents may then be lifted out onto the plate and the paper removed from the table and discarded.

EACH SERVING PROVIDES:
218 calories, 8g protein, 2g fat, 4g dietary fiber
42g carbohydrate, 55mg sodium, 0mg cholesterol

Pizza with Fresh Basil, Capers, and Pine Nuts

ALMOST INSTANT

Here is a simple, delicious, and superbly satisfying pizza. Its flavor and texture are light, so serve it with a hearty salad such as Rice and Lentils with Pimiento-Stuffed Olives (page 44).

YIELD: 4 MAIN-DISH SERVINGS

1 12-inch pizza crust
½ pound fresh pear tomatoes (about 3 medium)
⅓ cup chopped fresh basil leaves
1 clove garlic, minced
⅛ teaspoon salt
2 tablespoons small capers, drained
2 teaspoons dried oregano, crushed
Several grinds black pepper
3 tablespoons pine nuts

PREPARE a pizza crust from the Basic Pizza Crust recipe on pages 222–223, or use a commercially prepared crust for an almost instant pizza. Place the uncooked crust on a round pizza pan or a baker's peel that has been sprinkled with cornmeal. Preheat a coal or gas grill to high, about 500 degrees F., or preheat the oven to 450 degrees F.

Cut out and discard the stem ends of the tomatoes, but do not peel them. Puree the tomatoes in a food processor with the basil, garlic, and salt. Spread the tomato sauce over the crust, leaving a 1-inch border free of sauce, then top the sauce evenly with the capers, oregano, and pepper. Transfer the pizza to the hot grill and cover the grill, or place it in the preheated oven. Bake for 10–12 minutes, until the crust is golden and the sauce is sizzling.

Meanwhile, place the pine nuts in a dry, heavy-bottomed skillet over medium heat. Stir or shake them around frequently, until they begin to turn golden brown. Immediately remove them from the pan and chop coarsely. When the pizza is cooked, distribute the toasted pine nuts evenly over the top and serve hot or at room temperature.

NOTE: The following nutritional data includes one 12-inch Basic Pizza Crust (pages 222–223).

EACH SERVING PROVIDES:
298 calories, 9g protein, 9g fat, 3g dietary fiber
48g carbohydrate, 308mg sodium, 0mg cholesterol

Pizza with Salsa Verde, Tomatoes, and Olives

ALMOST INSTANT

The piquant green sauce used here has the consistency and appearance of traditional basil pesto but is much lighter in taste. This version of the traditional Italian *salsa verde* pairs well with the flavor of a piquant Mediterranean olive like the calamata.

YIELD: 4 MAIN-DISH SERVINGS

1 12-inch pizza crust
1 cup fresh Italian parsley leaves
1 tablespoon extra-virgin olive oil
1 tablespoon capers, drained
2 teaspoons fresh-squeezed lemon juice
1 clove garlic, minced
Pinch salt
Pinch cayenne
½ small red onion, thinly sliced
¼ cup minced calamata olives

PREPARE a pizza crust from the Basic Pizza Crust recipe on pages 222–223, or use a commercially prepared crust for an almost instant pizza. Place the crust on a round pizza pan or a baker's peel that has been sprinkled with cornmeal. Preheat a coal or gas grill to high, about 500 degrees F., or preheat the oven to 450 degrees F.

Combine the parsley, olive oil, capers, lemon juice, garlic, salt, and cayenne in a food processor and puree until smooth and homogenous.

Spread the crust with the green sauce, leaving a 1-inch border free of sauce. Distribute the onion slices and olives evenly over the green sauce. Transfer the pizza to a hot grill and cover the grill, or place in the preheated oven. Bake for 10–12 minutes, until the crust is golden. Serve immediately.

NOTE: The following nutritional data includes one 12-inch Basic Pizza Crust (pages 222–223).

EACH SERVING PROVIDES:

308 calories, 7g protein, 11g fat, 2g dietary fiber
46g carbohydrate, 466mg sodium, 0mg cholesterol

POSH OUTDOOR PIZZA PARTY

• •

Artichokes Stuffed with Marinated
French Lentils, page 30

Pizza with Salsa Verde, Tomatoes, and Olives, page 216

Provençal Skewered Vegetables with
Balsamic Marinade, page 108

Mixed greens with basil vinaigrette

Chardonnay

Grilled Eggplant and Pepper Pizza with Baked Garlic

Eggplants and peppers are abundant during the late summer and early autumn, which is also the perfect season for cooking on the grill. Serve the pizza with a hearty Mediterranean-flavored bean or pasta salad and a fruity red wine.

YIELD: 4 MAIN-DISH SERVINGS

1 12-inch pizza crust
2 medium bulbs garlic
1 medium red bell pepper
1 medium green bell pepper
1 medium eggplant (about 1 pound)
1 tablespoon plus 1 teaspoon olive oil
2 tablespoons capers, drained
2 tablespoons minced fresh oregano leaves
Scant ⅛ teaspoon salt
Several grinds black pepper

PREPARE a pizza crust from the Basic Pizza Crust recipe on pages 222–223, or use a commercially prepared crust. Place the uncooked crust on a round pizza pan or a baker's peel that has been sprinkled with cornmeal.

Meanwhile, preheat the oven or a toaster oven to 350 degrees F. Rub off the outer papery skin from the whole garlic bulbs, but do not peel or break them into individual cloves. Use a clay garlic baker or wrap the bulbs in foil and bake 30–45 minutes. When the garlic bulb is very soft, remove it from the oven and set aside to cool. When cool enough to handle, remove the garlic from the skins by breaking off the individual cloves and squeezing them from the bottom. The garlic will slide out as a soft paste. Spread this evenly over the pizza crust, leaving a 1-inch border free of garlic. Preheat a coal or gas grill to medium.

Slice the peppers in half lengthwise and remove the stems, seeds, and white membranes. Cut the halves lengthwise into strips ½ inch wide. Remove the stem of the eggplant, but do not peel it. Cut the eggplant into ¼-inch slices from stem to base. Brush one side of the eggplant slices with ½ tablespoon of the olive oil and place the eggplant on the grill, oiled side down. Place the peppers in a grill basket or on a fine-mesh grill rack. Close the lid of the grill and cook 6 minutes. Brush the other side of the eggplant slices with the remaining ½ tablespoon of oil and turn over. Turn the peppers. Cover and cook about 5 minutes longer. The eggplant and peppers should be slightly charred and limp. Remove the vegetables from the grill and set aside. Increase the grill temperature to high, about 500 degrees F., while you assemble the pizza. (Alternatively, you may cook the pizza in a conventional oven that has been preheated to 450 degrees F.)

Evenly distribute the eggplant and peppers over the garlic-coated pizza crust. Add the capers, oregano, salt, and pepper. Drizzle with the teaspoon of olive oil and bake for 10–12 minutes, until the crust is golden. Serve immediately.

NOTE: The following nutritional data includes one 12-inch Basic Pizza Crust (pages 222–223).

EACH SERVING PROVIDES:
340 calories, 9g protein, 10g fat, 4g dietary fiber
57g carbohydrate, 310mg sodium, 0mg cholesterol

Pizza with Black Beans, Avocado, and Cilantro

ALMOST INSTANT

This meal is fun to prepare on a warm summer evening. The pureed black beans make a nice base for the chiles, olives, tomatoes, and avocado.

YIELD: 4 MAIN-DISH SERVINGS

1 12-inch pizza crust
1 cup freshly cooked or canned black beans, drained
$\frac{1}{4}$ cup bean cooking liquid or water
1 green onion, minced
$\frac{1}{2}$ teaspoon ground cumin
$\frac{1}{2}$ teaspoon chili powder
1 clove garlic, minced
$\frac{1}{8}$ teaspoon salt
A few grinds black pepper
1 can ($4\frac{1}{4}$ ounces) diced green chiles, drained
1 can ($2\frac{1}{4}$ ounces) sliced black olives, drained
$\frac{1}{2}$ cup minced fresh cilantro leaves
2 medium fresh tomatoes (about 1 pound), sliced
1 medium ripe avocado, sliced

PREPARE a pizza crust from the Basic Pizza Crust recipe on pages 222–223, or use a commercially prepared crust for an almost instant pizza. Place the crust on a round pizza pan or a baker's peel that has been sprinkled with cornmeal. Preheat a coal or gas grill to high, about 500 degrees F., or preheat the oven to 450 degrees F.

Place the beans and bean cooking liquid in a food processor with the green onion, cumin, chili powder, garlic, salt, and pepper. Puree until smooth. Spread this mixture over the crust, leaving a 1-inch border free of beans. Sprinkle on the chiles, olives, and cilantro, then arrange the tomato slices. Bake for 10–12 minutes until the crust is golden. Arrange avocado slices on the pizza in a pretty pattern. Serve immediately.

NOTE: The following nutritional data includes one 12-inch Basic Pizza Crust (pages 222–223).

EACH SERVING PROVIDES:

416 calories, 12g protein, 15g fat, 6g dietary fiber
61g carbohydrate, 459mg sodium, 0mg cholesterol

Basic Pizza Crust

Use bread flour or unbleached white flour for best results. The flour measure is given as a range because the exact amount will vary depending on the day's humidity and other conditions. The temperature of the water used to start the yeast is important—if it is too hot, it will kill the yeast; if it is too cold, the yeast will not be activated. A simple thermometer can be used to eliminate the guesswork.

YIELD: 2 12-INCH PIZZA CRUSTS

¼ ounce active dry yeast (1 envelope)
1½ cups lukewarm water (105–115 degrees F.)
2 tablespoons plus ½ teaspoon olive oil
½ teaspoon salt
3½–4 cups unbleached flour

PLACE the yeast in a large bowl and add the warm water. Stir with a wooden spoon to dissolve the yeast, then set aside in a warm place until creamy in appearance, about 15 minutes. Stir in the 2 tablespoons of oil and the salt, then add 2 cups of the flour. Stir to incorporate, using a large wooden spoon. The mixture will be very sticky at this point. Add 1 more cup of the flour and continue to stir until the dough begins to form a ball. Turn out onto a lightly floured work surface and knead the dough until it is soft and smooth, about 10 minutes, adding the remaining flour as needed, a bit at a time, until the dough is no longer sticky. Too much flour will result in a dry dough that can become a slightly tough crust, so don't add any more flour than necessary.

Lightly oil a large bowl with the ½ teaspoon of oil. Place the dough ball in the oiled bowl, turn it to coat the entire surface with oil, and cover the bowl with a clean dish towel. Place the bowl in a warm, draft-free place for the dough to rise until doubled in volume, about 1½ hours. (An unlit oven or warm cupboard works well.) After it has risen, punch the dough down with your fist or fingertips to press out most of the air.

Place the dough on a lightly floured work surface and divide it into 2 balls of equal size. Working with 1 ball at a time, flatten it with your hands into a circle about 4 inches in diameter and 1 inch thick. Now begin working from the center, pressing the dough outward with the heels of your hands. If the dough sticks to your hands, sprinkle lightly with flour. Push the dough into a 12-inch round that is slightly thicker at the edges. (Alternatively, you may use a rolling pin to spread the dough into a 12-inch round.) If you are making only 1 pizza, the remaining dough ball may be wrapped tightly in plastic and frozen for up to 3 months. Thaw the dough at room temperature for a few hours before rolling out as directed. When the dough is rolled out, proceed with the instructions provided with individual recipes.

EACH CRUST PROVIDES:
994 calories, 24g protein, 17g fat, 6g dietary fiber
168g carbohydrate, 543mg sodium, 0mg cholesterol

MORNING MEALS

MORNING MEALS

Creamy Fruit Smoothie

Mixed Fruit Smoothie

Potatoes with Paprika and Chiles

Pineapple Papaya Salad with Dried Apricots and Coconut

Rice Porridge with Gingered Blueberries and Toasted Nuts

Savory Porridge with Vegetables and Miso

Curried Tofu Scramble

Corn and Potato Cakes with Southwest Seasonings

Breakfast Burritos with Potatoes, Pinto Beans,
    and Guacamole

Fabulous French Toast

S OMETIMES THE CLOCK DEMANDS that we make do with toast or fruit for breakfast. When time allows, however, a more substantial morning meal can be a wonderful gift to ourselves and our families. And on weekends, we can relax and enjoy a leisurely brunch with friends.

Whether you breakfast alone or with loved ones, make your morning meal a special one. Here are some delicious dishes that awaken the senses and provide ample nourishment for beginning the day.

Creamy Fruit Smoothie

ALMOST INSTANT

This smoothie delivers good portions of protein, essential fatty acids, and minerals—everything needed for good energy production throughout the morning.

YIELD: 2 SERVINGS

2 cups plain or vanilla soy milk
1½ cups fresh or frozen berries or chopped fruit
1 large banana
¼ cup flaxseeds
1 tablepoon blackstrap molasses

PLACE all ingredients in a blender and puree for about 1 minute, until well combined and the flaxseeds are somewhat ground up. Add ice to the blender if you prefer a frosty cold smoothie. Pour into 2 glasses and garnish with a mint sprig, if desired.

EACH SERVING PROVIDES:
178 calories, 4g protein, 3g fat, 5g dietary fiber
36g carbohydrate, 139mg sodium, 0mg cholesterol

"ARE YOU FLAXING?"

The seeds of the flax plant *(Linum usitatissimum)* provide such important health benefits that "flax" has almost become a verb among the nutritionally savvy. Whole flaxseeds are high in lignans, a fiber compound that has been shown to provide protection against hormone-linked cancers, such as breast cancer. Flaxseeds also support efficient elimination. Whole or ground seeds can be sprinkled on cereal or grains, or added to smoothies. Flax oil is an excellent food for vegetarians, as it provides the health-promoting omega-3 fatty acids typically associated with fish oils. Flax oil is delicious on salads or steamed vegetables. Look for organic flaxseeds in the bulk bins at a natural-food store. Flax oil can be located in the refrigerator case, and should be refrigerated at home, as it oxidizes quickly when exposed to light, air, or warm temperatures.

Mixed Fruit Smoothie

ALMOST INSTANT

This smoothie makes a refreshing breakfast. Fruit provides quick energy, but it doesn't last very long. Snack on a few raw almonds or vegetables as the morning progresses.

YIELD: 2 SERVINGS

3 cups chopped mixed fresh or frozen fruit
⅔ cup fresh-squeezed orange juice
1 medium banana

PLACE all ingredients in a blender and puree for about 1 minute, until well combined. Add ice to the blender if you prefer a frosty cold smoothie. Pour into 2 glasses and garnish with mint sprigs, if desired.

EACH SERVING PROVIDES:

180 calories, 2g protein, 1g fat, 5g dietary fiber

45g carbohydrate, 6mg sodium, 0mg cholesterol

SMOOTHIES

Smoothies are instant meals that provide refreshing flavor and good nutrition. To enjoy the maximum nutritional benefit, sip them slowly rather than gulping them down. Make smoothies year-round with the fresh or frozen fruit of your choice. We almost always include a banana, to thicken the mixture and for a good dose of potassium.

Potatoes with Paprika and Chiles

ALMOST INSTANT

A delicious version of "country-fried" potatoes, this dish is low in fat and can be enjoyed as often as you like.

YIELD: 6 SERVINGS

2½ pounds red potatoes
1 tablespoon olive oil
3 cloves garlic, minced
1 medium yellow onion, diced
1 small red bell pepper, chopped
1 small green bell pepper, chopped
1 tablespoon sweet paprika
¼ teaspoon salt
A few grinds black pepper
2 teaspoons dried dill
1 can (4 ounces) whole green chiles, drained and chopped

SCRUB the potatoes and, without peeling, cut in uniform large dice. Put in a covered saucepan with 4 cups water and cook over medium heat about 15 minutes, until barely tender.

Drain the potatoes and set them aside. Meanwhile, heat the olive oil in a skillet over medium heat. Sauté the garlic, onion, and bell peppers with the paprika, salt, and black pepper for 10 minutes. Stir the potatoes into the skillet, along with the dill, green chiles, and ¼ cup water. Sauté 5 more minutes, stirring frequently. Serve hot.

EACH SERVING PROVIDES:
194 calories, 4g protein, 3g fat, 0g dietary fiber
39g carbohydrate, 222mg sodium, 0mg cholesterol

Pineapple Papaya Salad with Dried Apricots and Coconut

ALMOST INSTANT

The refreshing colors and flavors of this fruit bowl can bring a brightness to the winter breakfast or brunch table since the tropical fruits are available year-round. Buy the pineapple and papaya a few days in advance so they can ripen to perfection in your kitchen. Serve this salad with whole grain toast coated with a bit of almond butter.

YIELD: 6 SERVINGS

1 medium fresh pineapple (about 2½ pounds)
1 large papaya (about 1 pound)
2 medium barely ripe bananas
1 large tart, crisp apple (such as Granny Smith)
12 halves dried apricots (about 3 ounces), chopped
2 tablespoons fresh-squeezed orange juice
1 tablespoon fresh-squeezed lime juice
¼ cup flaked coconut

SLICE off both ends of the pineapple, then cut the pineapple in half crosswise. Holding the flat side of one pineapple half against a cutting board, use a sharp knife to slice off the peel in a downward motion toward the board. Peel the other half. Cut each half into lengthwise quarters and slice off and discard the tough core portion. Cut the quartered pineapple into small, uniform chunks. Place the pineapple in a large mixing bowl.

Cut the papaya in half lengthwise and scrape out the seeds. Peel the papaya and chop the fruit into uniform pieces about the same size as the pineapple chunks. Add the papaya to the pineapple in the bowl.

Peel the bananas and chop them into small uniform pieces. Core the apple and chop it into bite-size pieces. Toss the bananas and apple with the pineapple and papaya. Add the apricots, orange juice, and lime juice to the bowl and toss. Transfer to a pretty serving bowl.

Place the coconut in a dry, heavy-bottomed skillet over medium heat. Toast for a few minutes, stirring constantly, until the coconut is uniformly tan in color. Immediately remove the coconut from the pan, sprinkle it evenly over the fruit, and serve.

EACH SERVING PROVIDES:

186 calories, 2g protein, 2g fat, 4g dietary fiber
44g carbohydrate, 15mg sodium, 0mg cholesterol

RIPENING TROPICAL FRUITS

Typically, tropical fruits such as bananas, kiwis, papayas, mangos, pineapples, and avocados are picked and sold under-ripe. However, they will continue to sweeten after harvest. Keeping this in mind, purchase such fruits several days before you plan to eat them. Store them in a bowl or basket at room temperature, but out of direct sunlight. Kiwis, papaya, mango, and avocado are ripe if they feel slightly soft when gently squeezed. Bananas and pineapples aren't ready to use until their skin is golden rather than green.

Rice Porridge with Gingered Blueberries and Toasted Nuts

ALMOST INSTANT

This breakfast dish is nutritious, delicious, and beautiful in the bowl. If you don't care for ginger, or have none on hand, substitute ¼ teaspoon ground cinnamon. For an almost instant breakfast, cook extra rice when you prepare dinner the night before.

YIELD: 4 SERVINGS

½ cup chopped raw pecans or walnuts
3 cups unseasoned cooked brown rice
1½ cups fresh or frozen blueberries
¼ cup pure maple syrup
½ teaspoon grated fresh ginger

PLACE the nuts in a dry, heavy-bottomed skillet over medium-high heat. Cook, shaking the pan frequently, until they begin turning golden brown. Immediately remove the nuts from the pan and set aside.

Combine the rice and 2½ cups of water in a saucepan over medium heat and bring to a simmer. Simmer rapidly 5–10 minutes, stirring frequently, until a thick porridge consistency is achieved. You may create a smooth-textured porridge, if you wish, by puree-ing some or all of the hot rice in a blender or food processor before serving.

Meanwhile, rinse and drain fresh blueberries and place them in a saucepan over medium heat with the maple syrup and ginger. Cook about 5 minutes, until the berries pop and the juice thickens a little. If using frozen berries, rinse to remove any ice crystals, drain briefly, then follow the same cooking procedure.

Portion the porridge into 4 wide bowls. Add a portion of the berries to each bowl and top with toasted nuts. Serve hot.

EACH SERVING PROVIDES:

335 calories, 5g protein, 11g fat, 5g dietary fiber

57g carbohydrate, 17mg sodium, 0mg cholesterol

Savory Porridge with Vegetables and Miso

ALMOST INSTANT

This savory porridge is similar to the thick soups often served in Japanese homes for breakfast. It's a good way to use up leftover grains and provides lots of nourishment on a cold morning. You may substitute other vegetables—such as daikon radish and cabbage—if you wish. Simply multiply ingredients if you want the recipe to serve more people.

YIELD: 2 SERVINGS

1 teaspoon raw sesame seeds
1 small turnip, scrubbed and diced small
1 small carrot, scrubbed and diced small
2 cups unseasoned cooked rice, kasha, and/or millet
1½ cups slivered collard or mustard greens
2 tablespoons light-colored miso

P LACE the sesame seeds in a dry, heavy-bottomed skillet over medium heat. Cook, shaking the pan frequently, until the seeds are a uniform golden brown. Immediately remove them from the pan and set aside.

Place 2 cups of water, turnip, and carrot in a saucepan over medium heat. Bring to a boil and cook 5 minutes. Add the grains, reduce the heat to medium, and simmer 5 minutes, or until a thick porridge consistency is achieved.

Stir in the greens and cook until wilted, about 1 minute. Remove the pan from the heat and stir in the miso. Distribute the porridge between 2 deep serving bowls and top with the toasted sesame seeds.

EACH SERVING PROVIDES:

386 calories, 13g protein, 3g fat, 5g dietary fiber
79g carbohydrate, 792mg sodium, 0mg cholesterol

HOT CEREALS

• •

Cereal grains deliver carbohydrates, fiber, and hearty substance—a winning combination that will provide lasting energy. Especially during cold weather, hot cereal—or porridge—makes a satisfying breakfast. Fruits and sweeteners are popular additions to the basic porridge, but savory seasonings are a delicious option. Cook extra whenever you are steaming grains for dinner, and enjoy the leftovers in the morning, as described in our two unconventional porridge recipes.

Curried Tofu Scramble

ALMOST INSTANT

Scrambled tofu is a terrific choice when a hearty, high-protein breakfast is called for. Serve this dish with your favorite breakfast potatoes.

YIELD: 8 SERVINGS

1 pound firm tofu
2 tablespoons curry powder
2 tablespoons brown rice syrup
1 teaspoon ground turmeric
½ teaspoon salt
1 teaspoon cumin seeds
2 cloves garlic, minced
1 medium onion, finely chopped
½ cup finely chopped red bell pepper
½ pound button mushrooms, sliced (2 cups)
1 teaspoon dried oregano

WITH your hands, crumble the tofu into a large dry skillet. Whisk one cup of hot water with the curry powder, brown rice syrup, turmeric, and salt, then stir this mixture into the skillet. Bring to a simmer over high heat. When bubbling, reduce heat to medium and cook, stirring occasionally, until liquid has evaporated and tofu consistency is as you like it (moist and soft or dry and crumbly). This will take about 15–20 minutes.

Meanwhile, heat 2 tablespoons of water in a skillet over medium heat. Add cumin seeds, garlic, onion, and bell pepper and cook for about 5 minutes, then stir in the mushrooms and oregano and cook 5 minutes longer, until mushrooms have released their liquid and are tender. Combine mushroom mixture with tofu mixture and serve hot.

EACH SERVING PROVIDES:

140 calories, 6g protein, 4g fat, 2g dietary fiber
23g carbohydrate, 146mg sodium, 0mg cholesterol

RELAXED WEEKEND BRUNCH

Fresh mango or melon slices

Curried Tofu Scramble, page 238

Potatoes with Paprika and Chiles, page 231

Whole-grain toast

Coffee or spiced herbal tea

Corn and Potato Cakes with Southwest Seasonings

Once you discover potato pancakes, you will begin to invent versions to accommodate whatever ingredients you have on hand. Guy Hadler is credited with this combination, and it is one of our favorites. Your favorite salsa is a nice accompaniment. If you're using fresh corn, you will need to purchase 2 medium ears.

YIELD: 8 SERVINGS

2 pounds russet potatoes (about 4 medium)
¼ cup plain soy milk
1 cup fresh or frozen corn kernels
½ cup diced red bell pepper
¼ cup minced fresh cilantro leaves
¼ teaspoon granulated garlic
¼ teaspoon ground cumin
¼ teaspoon chili powder
⅛ teaspoon salt
Several grinds black pepper
2 teaspoons canola oil

PEEL and dice the potatoes. Place them in a medium saucepan, cover with water, and bring to a boil. Once boiling, cook for 8–10 minutes, until fork-tender. Drain the potatoes well, place in a bowl, add the soy milk, and mash them. Stir in the corn and bell pepper, along with the seasonings. Form into 2- to 3-inch patties.

Place a heavy-bottomed skillet over medium-high heat and lightly coat with some of the oil. Fill the pan with patties and cook 3–4 minutes, until golden. Turn and brown the other side. Place on a platter in a warm oven and cook the remaining patties, adding additional oil as necessary. You should need no more than a total of 2 teaspoons oil. Serve hot.

EACH SERVING PROVIDES:

111 calories, 2g protein, 2g fat, 2g dietary fiber
23g carbohydrate, 136mg sodium, 0mg cholesterol

Breakfast Burritos with Potatoes, Pinto Beans, and Guacamole

This is a wonderful brunch entrée. We like to accompany the burritos with a garnish of fresh melon slices and a side of salsa. Depending on the occasion, serve them with fresh citrus juice, beer, or margaritas.

YIELD: 4 SERVINGS

1½ pounds russet potatoes (about 3 medium)
1 tablespoon canola oil
1 teaspoon dried thyme
1 teaspoon dried marjoram
3 green onions, minced
1 cup freshly cooked or canned pinto beans, drained
4 large flour tortillas
2 medium ripe avocados
1 clove garlic, minced
2 tablespoons fresh-squeezed lemon juice
1 teaspoon low-sodium soy sauce
Pinch cayenne
1 tablespoon finely minced red onion
1 fresh pear tomato, finely chopped
1 tablespoon minced fresh cilantro leaves

PEEL the potatoes, rinse, and cut into uniform, bite-size chunks. Put them in a saucepan and cover with cold water. Bring to a boil over high heat, then reduce heat to medium-high and simmer for 5 minutes, until they are just tender but not falling apart. Drain into a colander. Heat the oil in a large skillet over medium heat. Add the thyme, marjoram, and green onions. Cook for about 2 minutes to soften the onion, then add the drained potatoes. Sauté for 15 minutes, tossing occasionally, until the potatoes are lightly browned. Add the pinto beans and heat through for about 5 minutes.

Meanwhile, preheat the oven to 300 degrees F. Wrap the tortillas in foil and place in the warm oven. Cut the avocados in half, remove the pits, and scoop the pulp into a bowl. Mash with the garlic, lemon juice, soy sauce, and cayenne. Add the red onion, tomato, and cilantro and stir well. Let the flavors blend at room temperature while you finish the burritos.

Lay the warmed tortillas on warmed individual serving plates. Evenly divide the potato mixture among the tortillas and roll them closed. Top with the guacamole and serve immediately.

EACH SERVING PROVIDES:

629 calories, 18g protein, 24g fat, 11g dietary fiber
89g carbohydrate, 132mg sodium, 0mg cholesterol

Fabulous French Toast

ALMOST INSTANT

This vegan version of French toast doesn't develop a crisp outer layer like the egg batter variety, but its flavor and texture are terrific. Serve with maple syrup and chopped nuts, or an easy-to-make fruit puree. This breakfast is also delicious with fresh chopped berries.

YIELD: 6 SERVINGS

8 ounces silken tofu
½ cup plain or vanilla soy milk
1 tablespoon maple syrup
¼ teaspoon ground cinnamon
⅛ teaspoon ground nutmeg
2 tablespoons canola oil
12 slices whole-wheat bread

PLACE the tofu in a blender, along with the soy milk, maple syrup, cinnamon, and nutmeg. Puree, then pour into a shallow bowl.

Heat 1 teaspoon of the oil in a well-seasoned cast iron skillet over medium high heat. Dip a slice of the bread into the tofu mixture; coat well on both sides. Place in the skillet and cook until browned, then turn, adding a bit more oil as needed. Repeat with the remaining slices. Serve immediately with your favorite topping.

EACH SERVING PROVIDES:
200 calories, 8g protein, 8g fat, 4g dietary fiber
26g carbohydrate, 315mg sodium, 0mg cholesterol

FRESH FRUIT SAUCE

The strawberry is the first fruit that comes to mind for this flavorful sauce, although it is wonderful when made with apricots, peaches, apples or other varieties of berries. Simply cut the fruit into about ½-inch chunks and combine it in a heavy-bottomed saucepan with an inch or so of water. Place over high heat until the mixture begins to bubble, then stir and reduce the heat to medium. Add a tablespoon or two of brown rice syrup or maple syrup, if desired. Serve warm over French toast, pancakes, or tapioca pudding. Or pour it over your favorite cake, in place of frosting.

SANDWICHES
AND WRAPS

* * * * * * * *

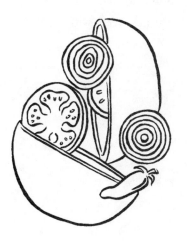

* * * * * * * *

SANDWICHES AND WRAPS

Tofu Salad with Water Chestnuts, Ginger, and Cilantro

Black Bean and Basmati Rice Burgers

Curried Eggplant and Garbanzo Patties

Tofu Patties with Dill and Toasted Sesame Seeds

Marinated Tempeh with Papaya Salsa

Grilled Vegetable and Rosemary Spread on Lavosh

Grilled Portobello Mushroom Sandwich

Grilled Eggplant Puree in Pocket Bread with
   Lemon Tahini Sauce

Tempeh, Salsa, and Avocado Wrap

Italian Rice and Veggie Wrap

Curried Bulgur and Garbanzo Wrap

Far East Wrap with Baked Tofu, Broccoli, and Hijiki

W E DELIGHT IN THE FREEDOM and simplicity of sandwiches and wraps. Raw or cooked vegetables, bean spreads, and patties—stuffed into or layered on bread—create a sometimes messy but always satisfying hands-on meal.

Everyone can customize a basic sandwich or burger with favorite condiments to create their version of the world's best sandwich. We've all learned an important sandwich lesson from Dagwood Bumstead: Anything goes.

Sandwiches and wraps also offer convenience, even when we make the fillings from scratch. Many of the recipes that follow can be made ahead and packed for a delicious lunch, and some can be frozen for later use.

The casual, easy-going appeal of the sandwich makes it a lunch or dinner favorite for children and adults. Here are some hot and cold sandwich and wrap options. Enjoy them throughout the year.

Tofu Salad with Water Chestnuts, Ginger, and Cilantro

ALMOST INSTANT

Think of this recipe as a template; you can experiment almost endlessly on the mashed tofu theme. How about a Mexican version with black beans, green chiles, and oregano? Or a Provençal version with tomato paste, fresh basil, and olives? As an alternative to the pita bread sandwich described in this recipe, tofu salad can be spread on chewy whole grain bread or mounded on a bed of greens with crisp crackers on the side.

YIELD: 6 SERVINGS

1 teaspoon raw sesame seeds
1½ cups unseasoned cooked brown rice
12 ounces firm tofu
2 teaspoons raw sesame tahini
2 teaspoons low-sodium soy sauce
2 teaspoons fresh-squeezed lemon juice
2 teaspoons grated fresh ginger
½ teaspoon dark sesame oil
1 clove garlic, minced
Pinch salt
Pinch cayenne
3 green onions, minced
⅓ cup grated carrot
⅓ cup minced water chestnuts
¼ cup minced red bell pepper
¼ cup minced fresh cilantro leaves
6 whole wheat pocket breads
1¼ cups finely shredded napa cabbage
1¼ cups mung bean sprouts

PLACE the sesame seeds in a dry, heavy-bottomed skillet over medium heat. Shake the pan frequently as the seeds toast. When they begin to brown and emit a nutty aroma, they are done. Immediately remove the seeds from the pan and set aside.

In a food processor, combine the rice, tofu, tahini, soy sauce, lemon juice, ginger, sesame oil, garlic, salt, and cayenne. Puree until well combined but still chunky; the longer you puree, the smaller the grains of rice will become, creating a smoother texture. Stir in the green onions, carrot, water chestnuts, bell pepper, and cilantro until well blended.

Cut each pita bread in half and gently open the pocket. Place some of the cabbage in each pocket, top with a portion of the tofu salad, then add some bean sprouts and sprinkle on a few toasted sesame seeds. Serve immediately, 2 halves per person. Refrigerate any leftover tofu salad in a covered container for up to a few days.

EACH SERVING PROVIDES:

287 calories, 14g protein, 6g fat, 5g dietary fiber
45g carbohydrate, 346mg sodium, 0mg cholesterol

Black Bean and Basmati Rice Burgers

Black beans and rice make a wonderful combination. Here we have paired them to create the perfect burger. Serve them with your favorite mustard or catsup. This recipe was inspired by a meal Guy Hadler had on one of his trips to Oklahoma.

YIELD: 8 SERVINGS

1 cup dried black beans
½ cup uncooked white basmati rice
¼ teaspoon salt
1 teaspoon chili powder
½ teaspoon ground cumin
Pinch cayenne
2 drops liquid smoke flavoring
¾ cup fine dry bread crumbs
2 teaspoons canola oil

8 whole grain burger buns
1 large ripe tomato, thinly sliced
8 butter lettuce leaves

ＳORT and rinse the beans, then soak them for several hours or overnight. Drain and rinse well, then place in a saucepan with 4 cups of water. Bring to a boil, then reduce heat to medium and simmer for about 1½ hours, until very soft.

Drain beans, reserving the cooking liquid. Return the drained beans to the pot. Add water, if necessary, to the bean cooking liquid to measure 2 cups. Add it to the pot along with the rice. Stir in the salt, chili powder, cumin, cayenne, and liquid smoke flavoring and bring to a simmer over medium-high heat. Reduce heat to low, cover, and simmer for 15 minutes, stirring frequently during the last 5 minutes. If rice is not yet tender, add another 1/4 cup water and continue cooking and stirring until it is absorbed. Mixture should be very soft and well combined. Remove the pan from the heat.

When the bean mixture is cool enough to handle, form into 8 patties. Coat with the bread crumbs. (If you are not serving 8 burgers, uncooked patties may be frozen between layers of waxed paper. Simply defrost before cooking.) Heat 1 teaspoon of the canola oil in a cast-iron skillet over medium-high heat. Cook the patties about 4 minutes per side, until golden brown. Add a little oil to the skillet as needed. You should need no more than 2 teaspoons total if using a well-seasoned cast-iron skillet.

EACH SERVING PROVIDES:

304 calories, 12g protein, 5g fat, 4g dietary fiber
46g carbohydrate, 331mg sodium, 0mg cholesterol

CAST-IRON COOKING

Our kitchens would not be complete without a selection of different-sized cast-iron skillets. They tolerate high heat and are virtually indestructible. Once they are "seasoned" (see manufacturer's instructions), they can be used to cook burgers, pancakes, quesadillas, and the like, using just a bit of oil. Clean them with hot water, very little or no soap, and dry them immediately by hand or on a hot burner.

Curried Eggplant and Garbanzo Patties

These slightly spicy patties make delicious and unconventional burgers that will be enjoyed by children and adults alike. Alternatively, serve the patties without the bun as a main course, with a grain side dish and a salad. They combine wonderfully, for instance, with the Beets and Greens with Bulgur and Miso Tahini Sauce (pages 148–149). Include a lemony green salad and mango chutney as a condiment, and you have a meal fit for company.

YIELD: 8 SERVINGS

1 large eggplant (about 1¼ pounds)
2 teaspoons raw sesame seeds
1 tablespoon plus ½ teaspoon olive oil
¼ cup minced yellow onion
2 tablespoons minced celery
2 tablespoons minced fresh parsley leaves
2 cloves garlic, minced
2 teaspoons curry powder
1 cup freshly cooked or canned garbanzo beans, drained
1¼ cups coarse dry bread crumbs
1½ teaspoons low-sodium soy sauce
1 teaspoon grated or minced lemon peel
Pinch cayenne

8 whole grain burger buns
⅓ cup mango chutney
1 large ripe tomato, thinly sliced
8 butter lettuce leaves

P REHEAT the oven to 375 degrees F. Peel the eggplant and cut crosswise into ½-inch slices. Place the slices on a steamer rack in a large saucepan over 2 inches of water. Cover, turn heat to medium-high, and steam 5–10 minutes, until the eggplant is quite soft.

Meanwhile, place the sesame seeds in a dry, heavy-bottomed skillet and toast over medium heat, stirring constantly, until they begin to brown and emit a nutty aroma. Immediately remove the seeds from the pan and set aside.

Heat the 1 tablespoon olive oil in a sauté pan over medium heat. Add the onion, celery, parsley, garlic, and curry powder and sauté 5 minutes, stirring frequently. Remove the pan from the heat and immediately add 2 tablespoons of water. Stir around quickly and set the pan aside.

When the eggplant is done, combine it with the garbanzo beans in a food processor. Pulse a few times to create a fairly coarse puree. Place in a bowl and add the sautéed vegetables, bread crumbs, sesame seeds, soy sauce, lemon peel, and cayenne. Stir until the mixture is thick and well combined.

Use the ½ teaspoon olive oil to rub down a baking sheet. Form the bean mixture into even-sized, somewhat flattened patties. (If you are not serving 8 burgers, uncooked patties may be frozen between layers of waxed paper. Simply defrost before cooking.) Place the patties on the oiled baking sheet and bake 30–35 minutes, until they are lightly browned on the top.

Assemble the burgers by spreading mango chutney on each of the buns. Top with an eggplant patty, tomato slice, and lettuce leaf and serve.

EACH SERVING PROVIDES:
299 calories, 10g protein, 7g fat, 3g dietary fiber
43g carbohydrate, 354mg sodium, 0mg cholesterol

Tofu Patties with Dill and Toasted Sesame Seeds

ALMOST INSTANT

These delectable patties can be served as an entrée with a simple mustard sauce or on whole wheat buns with your favorite fixings. The preparation is simple, and even picky children will love the results.

YIELD: 8 SERVINGS

½ cup uncooked bulgur wheat
1 tablespoon raw sesame seeds
8 ounces firm tofu
2 tablespoons arrowroot powder
¼ cup minced yellow onion
2 cloves garlic, minced
1 teaspoon dried dill
1 tablespoon low-sodium soy sauce
¼ cup minced fresh parsley leaves
Pinch cayenne
2 tablespoons canola oil

8 whole grain sesame seed buns

BRING 1 cup of water to a boil, then stir in the bulgur. Cover, reduce heat to very low, and cook for 10 minutes, until the water is absorbed. Remove from the heat and allow to sit, covered, for 5 minutes.

Meanwhile, place the sesame seeds in a dry, heavy-bottomed skillet over medium heat. Shake the pan frequently to toss the seeds as they toast. The seeds are toasted when they begin to brown and emit a nutty aroma. Immediately remove them from the pan and set aside.

Cut the tofu into ½-inch slices and pat them dry with a tea towel. Crumble tofu into a bowl and mix in the arrowroot powder, onion, garlic, dill, soy sauce, parsley, and cayenne. Add the cooked bulgur and mix until well combined. Form the mixture into eight 3-inch patties.

Heat ½ tablespoon of the oil in a cast-iron skillet over medium-high heat. Fill the pan with patties and cook about 4 minutes per side, until lightly browned. Place the cooked patties on a platter and keep warm. Use the remaining oil as needed to cook the remaining patties. You should need no more than 2 tablespoons total oil if using a well-seasoned cast-iron skillet.

EACH SERVING PROVIDES:

237 calories, 9g protein, 8g fat, 3g dietary fiber
27g carbohydrate, 274mg sodium, 0mg cholesterol

Marinated Tempeh with Papaya Salsa

The papaya salsa calls for dandelion greens. You may use the wild variety growing in your yard, or purchase them at the market. The salsa is the perfect accompaniment to the smoky-flavored tempeh. Serve these patties with steamed rice and a green vegetable or on a whole grain bun with the salsa and lettuce leaves.

YIELD: 4 SERVINGS

1 tablespoon dark sesame oil
2 tablespoons low-sodium soy sauce
2 tablespoons mirin
2 cloves garlic, minced
1 tablespoon grated fresh ginger
8 ounces tempeh

The salsa
½ ripe papaya
2 tablespoons minced dandelion greens
2 green onions, minced
¼ cup minced red bell pepper
1 clove garlic, minced
¼ teaspoon chili powder
1 tablespoon fresh-squeezed lime juice

4 whole grain buns

IN a small bowl, make a marinade by whisking together the sesame oil, soy sauce, mirin, garlic, and ginger. Cut the tempeh into 4 uniform, thin slices. Place the tempeh slices on a platter and drizzle evenly with half of the marinade. Turn them over and drizzle evenly with the remaining marinade. Set aside at room temperature for 30 minutes, turning occasionally.

To make the salsa, discard the seeds in the papaya half. Peel and cut the fruit into small cubes. Place it in a bowl and add the dandelion greens, onions, bell pepper, garlic, chili powder, and lime juice. Gently toss to combine and set aside.

Heat a cast-iron or heavy-bottomed skillet over medium-high. Add the tempeh slices, along with their marinade. Cook for about 4 minutes, until the tempeh begins to brown, then turn and brown the other side. If served as an entrée, pass the salsa. To serve as a burger, place the tempeh on the bun and top with salsa.

EACH SERVING PROVIDES:

330 calories, 17g protein, 11g fat, 3g dietary fiber
36g carbohydrate, 498mg sodium, 0mg cholesterol

SPLENDID SANDWICH SUPPER

• •

Marinated Tempeh with Papaya Salsa, page 258

Black-Eyed Peas, Corn, and Toasted Walnuts with
Spicy/Sweet Vinaigrette, page 46

Mixed Greens with Peas and Mustard
Miso Vinaigrette, page 34

Beer or iced tea

Grilled Vegetable and Rosemary Spread on Lovash

Lovash is Armenian cracker bread, most commonly sold with three large crisp rounds in a package. Some specialty stores in ethnic neighborhoods and some natural food stores will sell it "soft" rolled. If you cannot find the soft-rolled variety, follow the manufacturer's directions to dampen the crisp rounds. This spread is also delicious rolled in the Norwegian-style soft flat bread. This recipe makes 12 luncheon servings or 24 appetizer servings.

YIELD: 12 SERVINGS

2 pounds zucchini (about 6 medium)
¼ cup olive oil
2 pounds red bell peppers (about 4 large)
1 pound eggplant (about 1 medium)
1 pound yellow onions (about 4 small)
1 tablespoon balsamic vinegar
1 tablespoon fresh-squeezed lemon juice
3 cloves garlic, minced
1 teaspoon minced fresh rosemary leaves
¼ teaspoon salt
⅛ teaspoon ground black pepper
⅓ cup chopped calamata olives

17 ounces fresh lovash bread (3 large rounds)

PREHEAT a coal or gas grill to high. Remove the stem ends of the zucchini and slice lengthwise into thirds. Lightly brush the zucchini with a bit of the olive oil. Cut the peppers in half, discard the stems, seeds, and white membrane, then slice each half in thirds lengthwise. They do not need to be brushed with oil. Place the zucchini and peppers in a rack on the grill and cook about 15–20 minutes, turning several times. They will char slightly and become limp. Set the cooked zucchini and peppers aside on a plate.

Remove the stem end of the eggplant and cut the eggplant lengthwise into ½-inch slices. Brush lightly with a bit of the oil. Place the slices on the grill and cook 10 minutes, then turn and continue to cook about 10 minutes, until slightly charred and limp. Trim off the ends of the onions and peel them. Cut them in half crosswise and lightly brush with some of the oil. Place the onions on the grill with one cut end down. Cover the grill and cook for about 35 minutes, turning every 8–10 minutes to cook evenly. The onions are done when they are soft and slightly charred.

Meanwhile, bring the lovash to room temperature. Whisk together the remaining olive oil, balsamic vinegar, lemon juice, garlic, rosemary, salt, and pepper. Remove all of the vegetables from the grill and coarsely chop them. Place them in a food processor along with the olives. Pulse to chop, but do not puree. Pour in the oil mixture in a slow, steady stream, pulsing as you do so.

Lay the lovash rounds on the counter and spread the vegetable mixture evenly over them with a rubber spatula. For sandwiches, begin at one end and tightly roll up the bread into 3 large rolls. Wrap the rolls individually in waxed paper. Refrigerate for several

(continued)

(Grilled Vegetable and Rosemary Spread on Lovash, *continued*)

hours. Before serving, remove the paper and slice the rolls into ½-inch rounds. Arrange on a platter and serve.

For bite-size appetizers, tightly roll up the lovash from one side to the middle, then tightly roll up the other side to meet it. Slice between the rolls and wrap the resulting 6 rolls individually in waxed paper. Refrigerate and serve as described in the previous paragraph.

EACH SERVING PROVIDES:

214 calories, 6g protein, 8g fat, 2g dietary fiber

31g carbohydrate, 320mg sodium, 0mg cholesterol

Grilled Portobello Mushroom Sandwich

ALMOST INSTANT

Portobello mushrooms are prized for their rich flavor and firm "meaty" texture. For this mouth-watering sandwich, try to choose mushrooms that are about 5 inches in diameter.

YIELD: 4 SERVINGS

4 portobello mushrooms (about 1 pound)
¼ cup olive oil
4 sweet French rolls
½ large ripe tomato
4 large butter lettuce leaves

PREHEAT a coal or gas grill to medium-high. Remove the stem from each mushroom and set it aside for another use, such as soup stock. Gently brush the cap and gills of the mushrooms to remove any bits of dirt. Brush the caps with some of the oil and place the mushrooms, cap side down, on the hot grill. Cook for about 7 minutes, brush the other side of the mushrooms with a small amount of oil, turn, and continue to grill 5–7 minutes. Lightly oil the cut sides of each roll and place on the grill. Toast to a golden brown, about 2 minutes. Depending on the size of the mushrooms, they can be placed directly on the rolls, or they can be sliced to fit. Top with the tomato slices and lettuce; serve with mustard and tofu mayonnaise, if desired.

EACH SERVING PROVIDES:
284 calories, 7g protein, 14g fat, 3g dietary fiber
34g carbohydrate, 66mg sodium, 0mg cholesterol

Grilled Eggplant Puree in Pocket Bread with Lemon Tahini Sauce

The cardamom, cumin, and coriander blended with grilled eggplant create a delicious filling for Middle Eastern pocket bread. We enjoy these sandwiches for lunch or dinner. The filling is also delicious served as a salad atop lettuce leaves.

YIELD: 6 SERVINGS

The sauce
⅓ cup raw sesame tahini
3 tablespoons fresh-squeezed lemon juice
2 cloves garlic, minced
¼ teaspoon salt
¼ cup fresh minced parsley leaves

The filling
1 pound eggplant (about 1 medium)
1 tablespoon extra-virgin olive oil
1½ cups freshly cooked or canned garbanzo beans, drained
1 large cucumber
1 pound tomatoes (about 2 medium)
¼ teaspoon ground cumin
⅛ teaspoon ground cardamom
⅛ teaspoon ground coriander

6 whole wheat pocket breads

P REHEAT a coal or gas grill to medium. Place the tahini, lemon juice, garlic, and salt in a bowl with ¼ cup hot water and whisk until smooth. Whisk in the parsley and place the sauce in a serving bowl. Set aside at room temperature.

Remove the stem of the eggplant, but do not peel it. Cut the eggplant lengthwise into 1-inch slices. Brush one side of the eggplant slices with ½ tablespoon of the olive oil and place the eggplant on the grill, oiled side down. Close the lid of the grill and cook about 6 minutes. Brush the other side of the eggplant slices with the remaining ½ tablespoon of oil, turn, and cook an additional 5 minutes. Remove the eggplant from the grill. When it is cool enough to handle, chop the eggplant coarsely. Place the eggplant and garbanzo beans in a food processor and puree.

Peel the cucumber and slice it into quarters, lengthwise. Cut out and discard the seeds, then cut the cucumber into ¼-inch slices. Core the tomatoes and dice them. Gently combine the cucumber and tomatoes in a large bowl. Add the eggplant mixture and toss until well distributed. In a separate small bowl, toss together the cumin, cardamom, and coriander, and stir the spices into the eggplant puree.

Cut each pita bread in half and gently open the pocket. Fill each pocket with a portion of the eggplant mixture. Serve immediately, passing the sauce.

EACH SERVING PROVIDES:

350 calories, 13g protein, 13g fat, 8g dietary fiber

48g carbohydrate, 383mg sodium, 0mg cholesterol

Tempeh, Salsa, and Avocado Wrap

ALMOST INSTANT

This mixture of Asian and Southwestern ingredients makes a delightful wrap. Enjoy these tasty wraps with a salad for dinner, or for an easy-to-take-along lunch. Any leftover filling can be kept in the refrigerator for up to three days, then wrapped in a tortilla and enjoyed as a meal on the run. The salsa can be either homemade or a fresh super-market variety.

YIELD: 6 WRAPS

8 ounces tempeh
6 tablespoons mirin
2 tablespoons canola oil
1 medium yellow onion, diced
½ cup fresh or frozen corn kernels
1 cup fresh salsa
1 avocado, diced
6 large flour tortillas or whole wheat chapatis

CUT the tempeh into ½-inch cubes. Heat the mirin and oil in a skillet over medium-high heat and add the onion. Sauté for 3–4 minutes, until beginning to soften, then add the tempeh and cook for 8–10 minutes, stirring occasionally. Add the corn, salsa, and avocado, stir to combine, then continue to cook for 6–8 minutes until the liquid evaporates.

Meanwhile, wrap the tortillas in a tea towel and place in a 250 degrees F. oven until heated through, about 5 minutes. Lay a tortilla on the work surface and mound ⅙ of the mixture in the center. Fold in the sides and roll up tightly. Fill the remaining tortillas in the same fashion. Serve immediately. (Leftovers may be wrapped in plastic, refrigerated, and enjoyed the following day.)

EACH WRAP PROVIDES:
435 calories, 15g protein, 18g fat, 8g dietary fiber
52g carbohydrate, 379mg sodium, 0mg cholesterol

IT'S A WRAP!

"Wrap" is a term recently coined to describe any combination of savory ingredients rolled into a tortilla or chapati to create a satisfying casual meal. This trend has really taken off in some parts of the country. To meet the newly created demand for appropriate wrappers, super-size tortillas—some of them creatively seasoned—are now showing up in supermarkets. Seek them out or use a large whole wheat flour tortilla or chapati.

Italian Rice and Veggie Wrap

An Italian-inspired *salsa verde* provides the flavor punch in this rice and vegetable wrap, which is perfect as a lunch or casual dinner entrée. This recipe makes 12 smallish wraps, so will feed 6–12 people, depending on the other dishes you will be serving.

YIELD: 12 WRAPS

1½ cups uncooked short-grain brown rice
3 cups lightly packed fresh Italian parsley leaves
3 tablespoons extra-virgin olive oil
3 tablespoons drained capers
2 tablespoons fresh-squeezed lemon juice
4 medium cloves garlic, minced
¼ teaspoon dried red chile flakes
Pinch salt
½ cup diced celery
4 green onions, minced
1 cup diced red bell pepper
12 large flour tortillas or whole wheat chapatis

PLACE 3 cups of water in a saucepan that has a tight-fitting lid. Bring to a boil over high heat, then add the rice. Stir, reduce the heat to very low, cover the pan, and simmer for 45 minutes. Turn off the heat and allow the pan to sit for 5 minutes without disturbing the lid.

Meanwhile, for the sauce, combine the parsley, olive oil, capers, lemon juice, garlic, chile flakes, and salt in a food processor or blender and puree until smooth.

Wrap the tortillas in a tea towel and place in a 250 degrees F. oven until heated through, about 5 minutes. Add the parsley sauce to the rice, along with the celery, green onions, and bell pepper. Stir well to combine. Lay a tortilla on the work surface and mound $\frac{1}{12}$th of the rice mixture in the center. Fold in the sides and roll up tightly. Fill the remaining tortillas in the same fashion. Serve immediately. (Leftovers may be wrapped in plastic, refrigerated, and enjoyed the following day.)

EACH WRAP PROVIDES:

334 calories, 9g protein, 9g fat, 6g dietary fiber

53g carbohydrate, 242mg sodium, 0mg cholesterol

Curried Bulgur and Garbanzo Wrap

These wraps have a delicious Middle-Eastern flavor and are quite hearty. For an almost instant wrap, you can use any left-over cooked grain in place of the freshly cooked bulgur.

YIELD: 4 WRAPS

1½ cups Homemade Vegetable Stock (see NOTE)
¾ cup uncooked bulgur wheat
1 teaspoon dried oregano
¼ teaspoon ground cumin
¼ teaspoon ground coriander
4 large flour tortillas or whole wheat chipatis
2 tablespoons toasted sesame tahini
¼ cup fresh-squeezed lemon juice
2 tablespoons water
1 clove garlic, minced
½ teaspoon salt
⅛ teaspoon cayenne
1 cup cooked garbanzo beans
½ cup diced cucumber
1 medium tomato, diced
¼ cup minced fresh cilantro

BRING the stock to a boil in a large saucepan and add the bulgur, oregano, cumin, and coriander. Return to a boil, cover the pan, reduce the heat to very low, and cook 10 minutes. Turn off the heat and let the pan sit, without disturbing the lid, for at least 5 minutes.

Meanwhile, wrap the tortillas in a tea towel and place in a 250 degrees F. oven until heated through. For the sauce, whisk together the tahini, lemon juice, water, garlic, salt, and cayenne.

When the bulgur is ready, lay a tortilla on the work surface and mound ¼ of the bulgur mixture in the center. Add ¼ of the garbanzos, cucumber, tomato, and cilantro. Drizzle evenly with ¼ of the sauce. Fold in the sides and roll up tightly. Fill the remaining tortillas in the same fashion. Serve immediately. (Leftovers may be wrapped in plastic, refrigerated, and enjoyed the following day.)

NOTE: If you do not have Homemade Vegetable Stock on hand, make some according to the directions on page 84, or dissolve ½ large low-sodium vegetable broth cubes in 1½ cups of hot water.

EACH WRAP PROVIDES:
496 calories, 16g protein, 13g fat, 11g dietary fiber
83g carbohydrate, 869mg sodium, 0mg cholesterol

Far East Wrap with Baked Tofu, Broccoli, and Hijiki

ALMOST INSTANT

This exotic combination of ingredients is absolutely delicious. The hijiki seaweed may be considered optional, if unavailable. However, sea vegetables provide such a boost of minerals and amino acids that we strongly encourage you to begin incorporating them into your cooking.

YIELD: 4 WRAPS

¼ cup dried hijiki seaweed
4 large flour tortillas or whole-wheat chapatis
2 cups small broccoli florets
1 large carrot
1 tablespoon fresh-squeezed lemon juice
6 ounces silken tofu
2 teaspoons dark sesame oil
1 tablespoon grated fresh ginger
1½ teaspoons soy sauce
4 ounces baked tofu, thinly sliced (see NOTE)
1⅓ cups cooked brown rice

PLACE the hijiki in a medium bowl and pour 2 cups of boiling water over it. Soak to reconstitute for 15 minutes. Lift the hijiki from the water, leaving behind any sand that may have settled on the bottom of the bowl. Rinse under cold water and coarsely chop.

Meanwhile, wrap the tortillas in a tea towel and place in a 250 degrees F. oven until heated through, about 5 minutes. Steam the broccoli for about 5 minutes, until fork tender. Grate the carrot and combine it with the lemon juice in a small bowl.

For the sauce, place the silken tofu in a blender with the sesame oil, ginger, soy sauce, and 2 tablespoons of water. Puree until smooth.

Lay a tortilla on the work surface and mound ⅓ cup of the rice in the center. Add ¼ of the baked tofu slices, broccoli, hijiki, and carrot. Drizzle evenly with ¼ of the sauce. Fold in the sides and roll up tightly. Fill the remaining tortillas in the same fashion. Serve immediately. (Leftovers may be wrapped in plastic, refrigerated, and enjoyed the following day.)

NOTE: Use a prepared baked tofu from the natural-food store, or make your own according to the directions on page 6.

EACH WRAP PROVIDES:
374 calories, 15g protein, 16g fat, 4g dietary fiber
48g carbohydrate, 434mg sodium, 0mg cholesterol

SAVORING SEA VEGETABLES

Seaweeds, also called sea vegetables, have been enjoyed as food for centuries. They contain a very high concentration of important minerals and supply vitamin B_6, a nutrient generally lacking in vegetarian diets. Sea vegetables are sold in dried form at Asian markets and natural-food stores, and are reconstituted by soaking in hot water before using. Sea kelp—best known by its Japanese name, kombu—is traditionally used to season and mineralize broths. Kombu may be added to any soup or stock, and is reputed to calm the digestive storm some people suffer when eating legumes. Simply include a thick strip of the sea vegetable along with your beans and any other seasonings in the cooking pot. By the time the beans are cooked, the kombu will have completely tenderized and will disappear into the broth with a vigorous stir.

GLOSSARY OF SPECIALTY INGREDIENTS

Adzuki beans   These small, oval, rusty red beans have been enjoyed in Asia for thousands of years. They have a distinctive nutty flavor and retain their texture well when cooked. Look for dried adzuki beans at Asian groceries and natural food stores.

Arrowroot powder   This fine white powder, ground from the tuber of a starchy tropical plant, is primarily used as a thickening agent for sauces. It is available at natural food stores and some supermarkets, and is sometimes sold as arrowroot "flour." Dissolve it in cold water before adding it to hot liquid. In the proper proportions, it will thicken the liquid almost immediately. Overcooking can turn it gummy, so add it to a dish near the end of the cooking time.

Arugula   Deep green in color, this cruciferous vegetable is rich in beta-carotene and high in vitamin C. The small, flat leaves resemble dandelion greens and have a distinct peppery taste. Arugula is also known as rocket or roquette. It is easy to grow in the garden and is also widely available in markets.

Balsamic vinegar   An invention of the Italian province of Modena, this vinegar is uniquely rich, dense, and mellow. True balsamic vinegar is made according to ancient techniques and aged ten to fifty years in wooden barrels before bottling. Its unique flavor has no substitute.

Basmati rice   This aromatic rice is grown in India and Pakistan and is available in white and brown varieties. Its fragrance is rather nutlike while it is cooking, yet its flavor is almost buttery. Basmati is lower in starch than other long-grain rices, so its cooked consistency is light and fluffy. White basmati can be found in most grocery stores; the brown variety is available at natural food stores.

Brown rice syrup   Made exclusively from brown rice, water, and cereal enzymes, this syrup has a consistency similar to that of honey, but a much less intense sweetness. It is available at natural food stores.

Bulgur wheat   Bulgur is produced from whole wheat kernels that are steam-cooked, then dried and cracked into a coarse, medium, or fine grain. Because of the initial steaming process, bulgur requires less cooking time than cracked wheat.

Calamata olives   These succulent purple-black olives (also spelled kalamata) are native to Greece. They have an intense, piquant, and distinctly bitter flavor.

Cannellini beans   Also known as white kidney beans, cannellinis are mildly nutty in flavor and hold their texture well. They are a prominent ingredient in many classic Tuscan dishes. They may be purchased dried or canned at Italian groceries and some well-stocked supermarkets.

Cilantro   The fresh leaves of the coriander plant, this distinctive herb—quite common in Mexican and many Asian cuisines—is often sold as Chinese parsley. It is widely available in American supermarkets.

Couscous   Couscous traces its roots to northern Africa. Made from precooked semolina wheat, the tiny grains of couscous are added to boiling water or stock, which they quickly absorb. The result is tender, light, and fluffy—more similar in texture to a grain than to other types of semolina pasta.

Crostini   This Italian word refers to crunchy oven-baked or grilled toasts, which may be eaten with a variety of savory toppings.

Dark sesame oil   This thick, brownish oil is very aromatic. It is used more as a flavoring than as a cooking oil. Look for it in any Asian grocery store or well-stocked supermarket.

Dried tomatoes   Dried tomatoes have an intense flavor and a chewy texture. Different varieties are available—the driest ones may be extremely tough and should be reconstituted before using. Place them in a small bowl and cover with hot water for 15–30 minutes. Drain, reserving the liquid for soup stock, if desired.

Dry oil-cured black olives   These pungent, wrinkled black olives lend a distinctive bitter flavor to Italian-inspired dishes. They are available in gourmet food stores or in the delicatessen case at Italian groceries.

Epazote   Epazote is an herb popularly used in traditional Mexican dishes. It is easy to grow in North America and will survive year-round if brought indoors during the winter. Mexican markets, both north and south of the border, usually carry it fresh and sometimes dried.

Fennel   Fennel looks a bit like celery, with overlapping layers of stalks attached to a base, forming a thick bulb. Its foliage, however, is feathery, and the bulb is paler in color and more enlarged than celery. Fennel has a pronounced licorice flavor, unusual and delicious raw, mellowing to a delectable sweetness when cooked. It is widely used in Italian cooking and sometimes sold at the market as sweet anise or called by its Italian name, *finocchio*.

Filé powder   Filé powder is simply ground sassafras leaves, used as a flavoring and thickener in gumbo and other Cajun dishes. It is available in the spice section of most well-stocked supermarkets.

Focaccia   This particular type of Italian flat bread can be enhanced with any number of herbs and other savory ingredients, such as onions, garlic, and olives. Fruity olive oil is always a prominent flavor note in authentic focaccia.

Gaeta olives   These small, smooth, purplish-black olives are frequently used in Southern Italian cooking. Look for jars of them packed in brine at Italian markets.

Hijiki   A nutritious sea vegetable, high in calcium and iron, hijiki is sold in dried form in natural food stores and Asian groceries. It has a more delicate texture than many of its seaweed relatives. Seaweeds harvested from American coastal waters may be preferable to imported brands because domestic producers have demonstrated care in harvesting only from unpolluted areas. Don't be concerned about a white "dust" that appears on some dried seaweeds. It is harmless condensed salt that will disappear in the soaking process.

Hominy   Hominy is a large-kerneled, dried "flint" corn that has been soaked in lime water and boiled. The dried kernels soften and swell to create a unique flavor and texture. Hominy appears frequently in Mexican cuisine and is a classic food in the southern United States, where it is the basis for grits. It is available dried, but since the cooking process is time-consuming, we buy canned whole hominy, found wherever a good selection of Mexican foods is sold.

Kasha   Kasha is roasted, hulled buckwheat kernels that have been cracked into coarse, medium, or fine granules. This earthy grain has a rather strong, toasty flavor. It is widely available in natural food stores and some supermarkets.

Lentils   This category of legumes includes many varieties. In this book, we use small green lentils, sometimes termed "French lentils"; the widely available brown lentils most familiar to American cooks; and red lentils, favored in classic Middle Eastern preparations. Seek out the less common types at gourmet shops or ethnic specialty food stores.

Madeira   Madeira hails from the Portuguese island of the same name off the coast of Africa, where it is produced. The sweetest Madeira is made from Malmsey grapes. After pressing, the wine is stored and aged on the island, which has no cool cellarage. This seeming maltreatment actually makes the wine smoother and more pungent and is responsible for its rich mahogany color.

Marsala   This dark sherry-type wine was first produced by the Woodhouse brothers in Sicily. An excellent sipping wine for an apertif or dessert, Marsala is also a distinctive ingredient in many classic Italian dishes.

Millet   Millet is a mild, tasty, versatile grain, rich in iron. It is an ancient food that still figures prominently in the cuisines of Asia, Africa, and the Middle East. It is available in bulk at natural food stores or boxed at many supermarkets.

Mirin   Mirin is the sweet counterpart of the Japanese rice wine called sake. It is used extensively in Asian dishes. Look for it in an Asian specialty food store, or a well-stocked supermarket.

Miso   Some types of this salty, fermented soybean paste also have a mellow, sweet note. Miso contains active enzymes reputed to aid digestion. Add it to enrich a dish at the end of the cooking time; cooking miso will destroy the healthful organisms. We use mild light-colored miso, which is less intensely salty than the darker varieties. If your regular supermarket doesn't carry miso, purchase it at a natural food store or Asian grocery.

Natural granulated sugar   Natural granulated sugar is simply dried and ground sugar cane juice. It may be used measure for measure in place of conventional granulated sugar.

Orzo   Orzo is the rice-shaped semolina pasta common to Greek cuisine. Like other pastas, it cooks in lots of water and is drained before being sauced. It is available in any market with a good pasta selection.

Oyster mushrooms   Delicate in flavor and texture, these mushrooms (*pleurotus*) are sold fresh in many supermarkets, as well as at Asian groceries. They are pale brownish-gray in color and are edible in raw form but more flavorful when cooked.

Parchment paper   This heatproof paper is used for classic meal-in-a-pocket preparations called "en papillote." It is sold at supermarkets alongside aluminum foil and other standard kitchen wraps.

Pickled jalapeños   Although pickled jalapeños are milder than fresh, they still are hot. The seeds may be removed to further reduce the spicy bite. The pickling process adds a pleasant, piquant note to the peppers. Look for them in Mexican markets or well-stocked supermarkets.

Pine nuts   Pine nuts are the seeds harvested from the cones of the stone pine, common to the Mediterranean regions of Italy. These small, oval nuts have a creamy color and texture and a unique rich flavor. They are often toasted to intensify their nutty taste.

Polenta   Polenta, a staple of the Northern Italian diet, is ground dried corn, known as cornmeal to most Americans. Soft polenta dishes are usually made from fine yellow cornmeal, whereas the firm-style dishes call for the coarse yellow variety. Some Italian markets simply sell "polenta," which works for any type of preparation. Avoid commercially packaged cornmeal that includes additives—the unadulterated grain is required for good polenta.

Porcini mushrooms   This delicious field mushroom, *boletus edulus*, is especially popular with Italian cooks. Its flavor is deep, rich, and robust. The porcini is rarely available fresh in the United States, though it is readily available in dried form in Italian specialty food stores and gourmet shops.

Portobello mushrooms   These large mushrooms often measure 6 inches or more across. They are prized by Italian cooks for their rich flavor and "meaty" texture. Portobellos are particularly delicious when grilled.

Quinoa   Although technically the seed of a vegetable plant rather than a grain, quinoa looks like a grain and has similar uses. It is about the same size as millet and has a delicate, light flavor. Quinoa is considered a nutritional powerhouse, full of important minerals and very high in protein. Seek it out at natural food stores or gourmet shops.

Radicchio   A member of the chicory family, radicchio adds a unique, mildly bitter accent to salads and other dishes. Though different colors are cultivated, the most common variety in American markets is mottled purple and white.

Rice milk   A non-dairy liquid available in various flavors, rice milk is an alternative to dairy and soy milk. It is available in natural-food markets.

Serrano chiles   These hot peppers are typically glossy green. They are usually about 2–3 inches long and less than ½ inch wide. Before dicing them, remove the seeds if you desire a milder dish. Serrano chiles are popular in Mexican and Tex-Mex cooking.

Sesame tahini   Tahini is made from hulled raw or unhulled toasted sesame seeds that are ground into a paste. The resulting spread is similar in texture to peanut butter but with an intense sesame flavor. Most natural food stores carry it, as do Middle Eastern specialty markets. It is sometimes sold as sesame butter.

Shiitake mushrooms   The shiitake (*pasania cuspidata*) is increasingly available fresh as well as dried in well-stocked supermarkets and Asian grocery stores. Its distinctive, earthy flavor combines well with many seasonings, but particularly those of the Far East.

Soba   Soba are thin Japanese noodles typically containing buckwheat flour but also sometimes made with yam flour or flavored with green tea. The buckwheat content and price vary considerably from brand to brand. Experiment to see what you prefer. Soba is available at Asian groceries and many natural food stores.

Sorrel   Lemony fresh greens that lend a distinctive tart note to a dish, sorrel is easy to grow in the home garden. It is also available in well-stocked supermarkets, where it is usually displayed among the fresh herbs.

Soy milk   Soy beans are soaked in water, pureed, cooked, and pressed to create this rich milk-like liquid. It has a higher protein content than cow's milk and is suitable for many of the same uses. The different brands of soy milk vary in richness and flavor—some are even sweetened or flavored with vanilla for use in desserts or with cereals. Most brands now offer a reduced fat or "light" version, which is interchangeable with regular soy milk.

Tempeh   Produced from whole soybeans that have been fermented, tempeh is a high-protein food with a chewy, "meaty" texture and nutty flavor. It is available at natural food stores and some well-stocked supermarkets.

Tofu   Tofu, a high-protein food used extensively in the cuisines of Asia, is made from soy milk that has been coagulated to form curds. The process is similar to that used to transform milk into cheese. Its blandness makes it very versatile, as it will readily take on the flavors of many different seasonings. Tofu comes in various textures, from soft and silky to dense and chewy. It is readily available at supermarkets and natural food stores.

Tofu mayonnaise   Typically made with silken tofu, this eggless emulsion has a spreadable consistency similar to standard mayonnaise. Various brands are available at larger supermarkets and natural food stores. Sample different ones to discover your favorite.

Tomatillos   This firm, green fruit, about the size and shape of a standard cherry tomato, grows enclosed in a papery husk. It has a fresh, tart flavor essential in many traditional Mexican dishes, particularly sauces. Well-stocked supermarkets often carry the fresh fruit; canned tomatillos are usually available if fresh are not.

Wheat berries   The whole kernel of wheat, dried wheatberries may be cracked or ground, or cooked and eaten whole as a nutritious side dish. They are available at natural food stores.

Wild rice   Not technically rice at all, this seed of an American wild grass species has a wonderful nutty taste and chewy texture. Grades refer to the unbroken length of the individual grains but do not reflect improved flavor or nutritional value, so there is no harm in purchasing the more reasonably priced grades.

ALMOST INSTANT RECIPES

The following list is a guide to the recipes in this book that require 30 minutes or less to prepare, from start to finish. This earns them our Almost Instant designation, which appears under the titles on the recipe pages. Pizzas are included on this list because one can find good-quality prepared pizza crusts or frozen bread dough for pizzas at the supermarket.

In addition to these, this book includes many quick-to-prepare recipes not labeled Almost Instant because they require additional time for baking or marinating.

Almost Instant Recipes

••••

SUGGESTIONS FOR
FURTHER READING

Vegan meals are centered on grains and vegetables, just as nutrition experts recommend. A diet free of dairy, eggs, and meat contains no cholesterol, very little saturated fat, and an abundance of fiber and complex carbohydrates.

Over and above its personal health benefits, veganism is an environmentally and ethically sound dietary option. Such luminaries as Francis Moore Lappé and John Robbins have eloquently argued these points.

Those interested in exploring any of these issues in depth may wish to consult the following books.

Clark, Robert, ed. *Our Sustainable Table*. Berkeley, Calif.: North Point Press, 1990.

Colbin, Annemarie. *Food and Healing*. New York: Ballantine, 1986.

Edwards, Linda. *Baking for Health*. New York: Avery, 1988.

Haas, Dr. Robert. *Eat to Succeed: The Haas Maximum Performance Program*. New York: NAL Books, 1986.

Hagler, Louise and Dorothy R. Bates, eds. *The New Farm Vegetarian Cookbook*. Summertown, Tenn.: Book Publishing Company, 1988.

Kushi, Michio with Stephen Blauer. *The Macrobiotic Way: The Complete Macrobiotic Diet and Exercise Book*. Wayne, N.J.: Avery, 1985.

Lappé, Frances Moore. *Diet for a Small Planet* (20th Anniversary Edition). New York: Ballantine Books, 1991. Eggs and dairy products used in some recipes.

Lappé, Frances Moore and Joseph Collins with Cary Fowler. *Food First: Beyond the Myth of Scarcity*. Boston: Houghton Mifflin, 1977.

McDougall, John A. *McDougall's Medicine: A Challenging Second Opinion*. Piscataway, N.J.: New Century Publishers, 1985.

———. *The McDougall Program: Twelve Days to Dynamic Health* (with recipes by Mary McDougall). New York: NAL Books, 1990.

Murray, Michael. *The Healing Power of Foods*. Rocklin, CA: Prima Publishing, 1993.

Piscatella, Joseph C. *Choices for a Healthy Heart*. New York: Workman Publishing, 1987.

Rifkin, Jeremy. *Beyond Beef: The Rise and Fall of the Cattle Culture*. New York: Dutton, 1992.

Robbins, John. *Diet for a New America*. Walpole, N.H.: Stillpoint, 1987.

————. *May All Be Fed: Diet for a New World*. New York: William Morrow, 1992.

Sass, Lorna J. *Recipes from an Ecological Kitchen*. New York: William Morrow, 1992.

Shurtleff, William and Akiko Aoyagi. *The Book of Tofu*. New York: Ballantine, 1988. Eggs and dairy products used in some recipes.

Turner, Kristina. *The Self-Healing Cookbook*. Grass Valley, Calif.: Earthtones Press, rev. ed. 1989.

INDEX

Index
••••

287

Index
••••

Index
••••
290

INTERNATIONAL CONVERSION CHART

These are not exact equivalents: they've been slightly rounded to make measuring easier.

LIQUID MEASUREMENTS

American	Imperial	Metric	Australian
2 tablespoons (1 oz.)	1 fl. oz.	30 ml	1 tablespoon
¼ cup (2 oz.)	2 fl. oz.	60 ml	2 tablespoons
⅓ cup (3 oz.)	3 fl. oz.	80 ml	¼ cup
½ cup (4 oz.)	4 fl. oz.	125 ml	⅓ cup
⅔ cup (5 oz.)	5 fl. oz.	165 ml	½ cup
¾ cup (6 oz.)	6 fl. oz.	185 ml	⅔ cup
1 cup (8 oz.)	8 fl. oz.	250 ml	¾ cup

SPOON MEASUREMENTS

American	Metric
¼ teaspoon	1 ml
½ teaspoon	2 ml
1 teaspoon	5 ml
1 tablepoon	15 ml

OVEN TEMPERATURES

Fahrenheit	Centigrade	Gas
250	120	½
300	150	2
325	160	3
350	180	4
375	190	5
400	200	6
450	230	8

WEIGHTS

US/UK	Metric
1 oz.	30 grams (g)
2 oz.	60 g
4 oz. (¼ lb)	125 g
5 oz. (⅓ lb)	155 g
6 oz.	185 g
7 oz.	220 g
8 oz. (½ lb)	250 g
10 oz.	315 g
12 oz. (¾ lb)	375 g
14 oz.	440 g
16 oz. (1 lb)	500 g
2 lbs.	1 kg